Sporty Course

Memoirs of a World War II Bomber Pilot

SPORTY COURSE

Memoirs of a World War II Bomber Pilot

Jack Swayze

Sunflower University Press ®
1531 Yuma (Box 1009), Manhattan, Kansas 66502-4228

© 1993 by Jack Swayze
Printed in the United States of America on acid-free paper.

ISBN 0-89745-163-5

Cover: Jack Swayze (second from left, standing) and crew, 1943-1944.

Edited by Sa
Layout by Lor

358.4
SWA
1993

Swayze, Jack.
Sporty course,
memoirs of a World
War II bomber pilot.

Contents

Introduction	vii
Chapter 1	1
Chapter 2	5
Chapter 3	12
Chapter 4	17
Chapter 5	24
Chapter 6	32
Chapter 7	40
Chapter 8	47
Chapter 9	64
Chapter 10	72
Chapter 11	80
Chapter 12	87
Chapter 13	93
Chapter 14	103

Chapter 15	110
Chapter 16	117
Chapter 17	125
Chapter 18	134
Chapter 19	137
Chapter 20	142
Epilogue	146
Index	148

Introduction

I have combined my memories of World War II with the official record of the missions in which I participated, but I discovered that the official records reflected a war I did not recognize. The rules of recording and reporting war history insure a less than true account. Losses and flops that the enemy does not know, we will not print in military history — let the enemy find out if he can.

We record and report those items supporting our political and military leaders as heroes, and those reports and histories depict only a positive and favorable view of our actions in the war. Many missions did not go as briefed. Field orders required revision, hiding mission failures and mistakes. The crews who flew the missions and those backing them up from time to time made mistakes. Some were tragic; some saved missions.

I wrote first from my memory and impressions. My book may contain inaccuracies in dates and mission order since it is from memory, but I believe that my memory, my flight records, and my friends' accounts are more accurate than the official record.

I must emphasize that the men doing the fighting are our heroes, and the men who supported the fighters are heroes as well. I am sure that the men in Headquarters tried to do a good job; it was not an easy task. But too much credit has gone to the plan and to the various Headquarters; too little credit has gone to the people who carried out the orders.

The United States had many crew members who lost their lives or became prisoners of war because of a B-24 hardware deficiency. During "Theater Change," for example, the Depot removed the B-24 gas gauges because they were a fire hazard and unsuitable for use in combat. Instead, the B-24 gauges were hoses connected to glass tubes mounted on the fire wall of the flight deck, behind the pilot and copilot. But in war you should not have glass tubes of aviation fuel inside planes. The problem was not corrected during the war years and thus these tubes remained disconnected in combat. Crews flew unaware of how much fuel they had used or had yet available. Corrective action could have been taken with ease by using the B-17 electric gauges.

This is only one problem of many that brings little credit to the American aviation industry or to the many Headquarters accepting these conditions. It is but one example of mistakes that the combat personnel had to endure and circumvent to survive. The total dollar value of these mistakes is in the millions, and the Army Air Forces thus lost many lives.

Friends say, "Why did you not tell more of the humorous incidents that existed during the war?" I do tell some, but most events were not funny. They were tragic. World War II was just not a funny time. Relating humorous incidents destroys the whole focus of those years.

If we tried to list the problems and disagreements solved by the war, we would find it difficult. We should then consider this question: Was the war necessary? Might a more eloquent appeal to reason have resulted in not having to fight to solve the problems?

The United States must never again adopt war as a legitimate solution to international differences. But neither do I advocate disarmament. I do, however, advocate going the extra mile to negotiate. I do advocate avoiding show-of-force and battleship diplomacy. We do not need a supremacy of force bringing victory with sticks and stones, conventional weapons, weapons of mass destruction, or nuclear weapons.

Our nation must solve problems with other nations by peaceful means. The United States Congress can refuse to declare war. It should do so until convinced that the President has exhausted all other options to gain a peaceful resolution.

Before resorting to war, the actions of the enemy must be so heinous that they become totally unacceptable to civilized society. In addition, *all* free peoples must accept the war to stop the actions of the enemy. Then, and only then, should the United States go to war.

And when we reach this point, we must win. The free world should proceed without regret or hesitation. Only with swift and sure action will deterrence be effective. At that point, I believe that the United States must use nuclear weapons to insure minimal loss of life and limb to our own forces.

Given this conclusion, read about our air involvement and my experiences in World War II!

Chapter 1

This was a day of decision for my wife Jeri and me. I had been managing a produce brokerage business since the end of my third year at the University of Washington. The business had not worked out. I was back in the University finishing my final quarter, and like most young people, I was in a hurry. When young, boys are always in a hurry. They have no tangible destination, but they're in a hurry to get there.

I took a job with the Paramount Theater as a doorman and arranged with the Dean of my college to write a thesis for eight credit hours. This would allow me to finish my degree in two quarters instead of three.

It was Sunday morning, 7 December 1941. I sat at the kitchen table typing on my thesis. I had completed a rough draft and was beginning a final version.

Jeri had gone over to the little store across the street to buy groceries. We had one son and another on the way; these were the pressures for me to hurry.

Jeri burst in saying, "Japan has attacked Pearl Harbor in Hawaii." I turned on the radio and we listened. People on the West Coast feared that the Japanese would attack, that Pearl Harbor was the prelude to an invasion on our coast.

Jeri and I discussed the situation a long time that night and believed that I had to get into war work with the military. Though my father had been helping us financially, we needed to become independent.

On Monday morning, I rode out to the old Ford Assembly Plant, across the street from Boeing Field. It was the home of the Quartermaster Depot for the Ninth Corps.

Because I had had a good background in produce, they put me to work at once. I received a temporary Civil Service rating and went to work filling requisitions from field units primarily for food items. I continued to work nights and weekends at the theater; and between the two jobs, we were able to meet our needs.

My life had begun with my being left on the steps of an orphanage in Spokane, Washington. From there I had been adopted and raised with a sister, also an orphan. I was one of the lucky ones, getting adopted — many were not.

Now here I was, trying to raise a family of my own. With a second baby about to arrive, Jeri and I looked for and found a larger apartment. Jeri had lost her father very early in life, and her Mother had moved in with us. She helped with the baby, and with the expenses.

My draft classification was 3E, meaning that I would not get drafted for quite a while. But I didn't feel that my work at the Quartermaster Depot was anything to hang my hat on for a lifetime profession. It just didn't amount to that much, and I found that we were all about to be frozen in our positions for the duration.

Each day at noon I would eat my lunch where I could watch the B-17 Flying Fortresses and the P-38 Lightnings take off from the Boeing Field on their way to war. They captivated and preoccupied me. The B-17 was my favorite, but I saw a few P-38s from Paine Field in Everett, Washington, coming and going, too. I knew then that I wanted to fly.

A Captain working at the Depot had married one of Jeri's sorority sisters, and he and I met often at noon to talk about flying. He was awaiting his orders to attend flying school and told me about the Aviation Cadet program, recommending that I take the exams. He said, "The Quartermaster will release you." But I had to move fast.

I talked to Jeri, and she suggested I try for the airlines first. I applied to United and was sent to San Francisco for testing. They made me an offer to go to work in Seattle in reservations. That was better than where I was, but I wanted to fly. So I took the exams for Aviation Cadet and passed with no problem. I felt that this was a chance to become a pilot; I could always fly with the airlines after the war. At that age I didn't think seriously about the likelihood of getting killed in the action; that possibility did not occur to me.

At the same time, my good friend, Sperling Boutelle, returned from a job in Alaska. He had served a tour in the Navy while I had gone to college, and he was re-enlisting.

Ninth Corps area covered everything from San Francisco north to include all of Alaska. Our section in the Depot grew daily; anyone who applied was hired. Our job was to fill requisitions from stock in the Depot. If we considered an item essential but it was not in stock, we could purchase it. Anything else not in stock was back ordered.

We determined what was in stock by checking the machine-run inventory book. But in roaming around the Depot, I found that this inventory book was at least a week behind. Many items did not show in the inventory, though they were actually in the warehouse.

I began to fill requisitions from personal knowledge though the inventory showed none on hand. I did this especially for items requisitioned by units on their way overseas to combat zones. But very soon the powers in charge barred me from the warehouse area; I was constantly on the carpet for violations of policy.

No one knew what was going on. We did not know what the actual war situation was, though we knew we were losing on all fronts. The public was very much afraid. The government had rounded up Japanese citizens and had begun moving them into detention camps. The Japanese in the camps received decent treatment, and many went into the camps for their own protection as they were being attacked, in some cases, by mobs. The general public and the Japanese Americans had little mutual trust, as there was a gap due to language and cultural barriers.

At Pearl Harbor the Japanese had hit us with a cowardly blow. Except for the aircraft carriers at sea, our Pacific Fleet no longer existed. We had been losing many ships and men delivering war goods to Britain, but the United States had not prepared for war. However, the Axis — Japan, Germany, and Italy — was moving on all fronts and was winning all battles. Yet the American people at the time were not capable of thinking of winning — winning was a long way off; survival was the question of the day.

Some zealots were running around saying, "Give us a couple destroyers and two weeks and we'll beat the Japanese." Men making those ridiculous statements would never serve in any war.

About this time, a new Civil Service supervisor from Philadelphia had arrived at the Depot. He had been a long-time civil servant — overweight and smoked big black cigars constantly. He began to preach that the units shipping out had to learn that there was a war going on. The troops had to learn that they must make do with what they had. If they tried, they could survive well without luxuries. Of course, that was easy for him to say! He was as close to combat as he had any intention of getting.

Rumor had it that a freeze order on supplies had arrived upstairs in the Command section. That same day, I received a requisition from a unit going to the Aleutians; the men had underlined walnuts as the item they wanted most. However, the Depot did not stock nuts, and if we were to get walnuts, it could only be by local purchase. I coded the item for purchase and waited for the explosion. My new cigar-smoking supervisor called me at once and chewed me out.

"I don't care where they're going; you'll not buy walnuts. You'll substitute."

In the meantime, I had decided to request Aviation Cadet school, so I brought this policy to a head. I inserted "Grapenuts," knowing that the substitution would not be accepted. About mid-afternoon, I saw the Colonel commanding the Depot coming down the aisle toward me with some papers in his hand.

He stopped at my desk. "Tell me why you did this." I told him all about the actions of my cigar-smoking friend. I handed him my request for release to go to Cadets, and he approved it on the spot, wishing me well.

The Army enlisted me as a Private, unassigned. I would draw a Private's pay until there was room for me to begin flying school. And I still worked, when called, at the theater. Working there was good experience. The pay was not much, so everyone tried to increase his earnings. Many Sunday nights I would let the hat-check girl leave early and take the final break duties myself. The tip basket would be loaded with quarters and halves; I could make $20 in tips on the final break.

When my orders came for flying school, Jeri and I went to Kennewick, Washington, to visit my parents. I had two weeks before reporting, so I helped with the farm work while visiting. On the last night home, we were watching a news report about fliers killed in a plane crash. Dad looked up at me and said, "I fear we may hear such a report about you someday."

Dad was afraid of both the war and flying. But I believed that flying would be my future. I believed I could succeed. I knew that if the risk was too high, the adventure could end in disaster. But flying seemed to have a reasonable risk level for my needs. It also provided a chance to serve my country as a bonus.

When the day to leave arrived, I believed if I did my utmost, God would see me through the rough spots. I was not one for organized religion, but I believed God would judge what I did each day and keep me safe. Doing "right" always had a high priority in my life.

Chapter 2

Twenty-six cadets were in our car on the train headed for pilot training. Our destination was Santa Ana, California. On the trip south, we all became acquainted; we talked about flying and the war. None of us had any real knowledge of what lay in store for us, so most of it was pure speculation.

There was a variety of men in our group. Another cadet and I were married with families. We were all going to flight training for different reasons. But I seemed to be the only cadet on board looking for a military career. Some were going to avoid infantry service and would wash out. Many draftees were going to delay seeing combat, many just for the adventure. Others did not want to fly or to be in the war at all. And most of them would not make it through flying school. Those of us who wanted to fly worried that we might fail, but no one voiced that fear.

In our discussions about the war, most did not express strong feelings. That reflected the "fool's paradise" view of the world we Americans had. Only the old men who had actually seen combat in World War I had a realistic knowledge of war. The United States had entered World War I late, near its end. Exhaustion had already taken a toll on both sides, so a push was all it took to win. The United States provided that push, and the Allies won. But World War II was to be another story!

At any rate, I vowed not to fail in flying school. I feared the war would end before I could reach combat, and combat provided the only way I could realize my goal of a flying career.

We loaded on buses at Santa Ana for the short drive to the base, which was a base without airplanes. It was the Pre-flight Training Center for the Western United States. There were endless rows of barracks and fields of tents. It was a sea of khaki and green, created by uniforms, tents, and military equipment.

When we stepped off that bus, we lost our identity. We were then just "cadet" or "mister." Mister was *not* a term of respect; rather it was used to make us realize we were at the bottom. From there, we could only go up. We learned that our body, mind, and soul belonged to Uncle Sam. The Army could do with us anything it wanted. Physical examinations, ground school, kitchen police, athletics, tests, and drill went on from first light until well after dark.

Six weeks of restriction to the post's cadet area became law. We saw an occasional P-38 flying from the nearby Army airfield, but that was as near as we got to an airplane in Pre-flight training.

We received extensive physical examination, far more thorough than the enlistment physical. The various medical findings were then compared and numbers, if either too high or too low, would drop you from flying as a pilot. It hurt morale to see so many failing to meet those physical formulas, and we wondered if the formulas were sound. I very much doubted their validity. Later the military did stop using them, but many young men had already washed out of pilot training.

I made friends with a young man who had a pilot's license for seaplanes. We had met on the train. Assignments were given strictly by the alphabet, resulting in our placement in different tents. However, we did manage to get together in off-hours and compare notes. Everything we did at Santa Ana was done according to alphabetical order. We all yearned for a name beginning with "A." A name like Aagard would have been heaven; names like Ziegler were names everyone pitied.

We first received a heavy dose of ground school instruction. Flight school was not going to be all fun and games. We had a lot to learn and precious little time. Some were beginning to wash out because of academic failure. And between the academic and the physical washouts, we feared dismissal more each day. We wondered if any of us would ever fly.

I was living with a bunch of New York recruits; some had never walked on anything but pavement, and there we were in the orange-grove area of southern California! A farm boy like me from Washington State working alongside fellows from New York could create problems. The cultures from different sections of the nation were interesting and distinct, and it was quite an adjustment.

One particular noon a Lieutenant came over and asked if any of us had a driver's license. That sounded as if it might be a chance to get off restriction. Several of us yelled, "I do!"

Chapter 2

The Lieutenant said, "Now, isn't that friendly. You guys drive your rears over to those new tents and scrub all the floors for the new arrivals due tonight."

It only took one experience to teach me never to volunteer. They have a saying in the military: "Keep your mouth shut, your bowels open, and never volunteer." If what you were to do actually was a good deal, it would have gone to some "fair-haired boy," not to one of us.

Another amusing incident typical of Army life occurred one night when our Squadron had guard duty. I drew a post on the corner of the tent area and was to patrol our road on foot. At about dusk, a jeep appeared driven by a First Lieutenant. He stopped and told me to check something. I did not understand what he said, and asked him to repeat the order.

He exploded, "Mister, how long you been in this Army? Just do what we tell you. Do it when we tell you. Get it done now!" Then he threw the jeep into gear and drove off.

I had to do something, so I went through my area, calling out incoherent words. "Get the Nitchen and the Gritchen out, now."

When anyone would ask, I repeated what the Lieutenant said. "How long have you been in this Army? Get it done and done quick!" I would yell.

This started a flurry of activity. Some raised or lowered the flaps on their tents. Some tried to tighten their tent stakes and pegs. Others dug new run-off ditches. Everyone did something. No one, especially me, had the vaguest idea what the Lieutenant had wanted, and since he did not return, I never found out what was to be done. Maybe he didn't know either.

That same night, a friend from New York was on guard duty at the base entrance. Charlie had instructions to stop each vehicle and have the driver turn on the dome light. Then with the light on, he was to check each identity card, matching the face with the picture.

A jeep came along in the middle of the night, probably driven by the same Lieutenant I had met earlier. Charlie said, "Turn on your dome light and show your identification!" After a verbal battle, he learned that jeeps did not have dome lights.

A cadet had no leeway to think. Deciding on an answer to a situation for which there was no order or rule could result in elimination from the program. That was training? The washout fear in cadet life grew and threatened to consume us.

After five of the six weeks of restriction, we received a bonus one Saturday night. We were allowed to go to a field canteen and drink 3.2 beer. It was a time to have fun, tell tales, and sing songs. It was good for our morale. We couldn't get drunk on the beer, because our stomachs just couldn't hold enough for us to get really high. But we could sure get sick!

On the following day, it was back to the old routine. We got up at dawn, picked up rocks from a pile, and scattered them all around. Then on the next day, we picked them up and stacked them in a pile. We went through the same routine again and again.

We spent time in ground school and athletics. We went to the ocean for swimming tests. The waves off Laguna Beach were severe, and the water was cold.

On the beach we fired the Thompson submachine gun. I soon learned to handle the gun by starting at the lower left of any figure and firing short bursts.

All restrictions ended the following week. We would be able to leave the base, so we were going to Los Angeles that Saturday afternoon. We had to be back for parade at noon on Sunday.

Most of us spent our time in bars because there was nothing else to do. We couldn't afford to rent rooms, even if there had been any available. We ended up trying to get some sleep in chairs in the lobby of a hotel. Sailors, soldiers, and marines occupied all the seats. Charlie Rybos and I were together, sleeping in a lobby. When we woke up, we saw an old man sweeping the floor; we commented on that, then dozed off again.

When we next awoke, there was a small elderly lady sweeping the floor. Charlie and I looked at each other. We were thinking, "Have we slept through until Monday?" If we had, we would be washouts for sure. We raced outside and bought a paper to find out what day it was. It was Sunday, thank God. So we had a cup of coffee and then waited for the bus back to Santa Ana.

The Sunday parade was for a purpose unknown to us; we used to debate its usefulness. All Squadrons competed, so we decided it was just a hangover from the Infantry and the Horse Cavalry. But the winners received privileges, and we won more than our share. We gained pride in our Squadron by winning. After the night off, however, the hot California sun was torture. There were long periods of standing at attention or parade rest.

All of those unlucky enough to faint washed out of pilot training. The Army picked up a lot of candidates for navigation and bombardier training from those who couldn't make it through the parade.

Another area of much discussion for the cadets was the routine picking up and piling of rocks. Why did we have to do this ridiculous task? It only seemed to delay our getting ready to fly and fight. Was it to teach blind obedience to orders? Or did the Army entertain hidden reasons? None of us could come up with a reasonable explanation other than the blind obedience.

Those permanently assigned to the post had a racket. They designated someone to the pay lines, and we each had to give a dollar for "lawn seed." Thousands of cadets went through Santa Ana. If each paid a dollar every payday while there, someone was making big money. We knew that the American taxpayers paid for any real lawn seed, but no one wanted to risk washout by complaining. Much later, an investigation uncovered the illegal

Chapter 2 9

activity. Officers involved got fined, but the cadets didn't get their dollars back.

The time arrived to leave for Primary training. Rumors spread about how to get the school we wanted. One was that the choice bases would go to companies that made a cash donation to their Company Commander.

Our company had a meeting. Some cadets opposed making a donation, but most favored giving it a shot. We appointed our acting Cadet Leader to approach our Company Commander. He reported back to us that the Commander said he could get us our choice, but a donation to help pay off the mortgage on his farm would be helpful. We chipped in ten bucks apiece, resulting in $500 for the Commander's mortgage.

The graft was wrong, but there was nothing we could have done about it. If we complained, we would wash out and would be transferred to an infantry combat unit. We dared not upset the apple cart.

When our orders finally arrived, we had gotten our choice — Ontario, California. All of us wanted to move on to flying school.

Ontario was a neat little school. The base was clean. We shared connecting two-man rooms, and the four men shared the bath between. It was a welcome setup after the open-bay barracks and tent city in Pre-flight. The Ontario flight line was a concrete ramp with strings of aircraft. Even the little yellow Stearman aircraft looked neat in their rows.

Besides getting our pick of bases, we also received a most welcome bonus. The day before our arrival, a member of the upper class came down with scarlet fever. His entire class was quarantined and couldn't come into our area and pick on any of us.

Ontario was formerly a private flying school (Cal Aero Academy). The Army had contracted the school for pilot training, and the instructors were civilians, except for a few Army Check Pilots.

My instructor, Orlo Watson, had flown more than 4,500 hours, some in shows all around the country, including Tex Rankin's Flying Circus. He had made the fair circuit and had participated in competitive flying. This beat having an Army instructor, especially one who had just graduated a class or two earlier. Watson was an outstanding man, someone a person would want for a friend, not just an instructor. It had been worth the money we had "donated" to get to Ontario.

Watson believed that anyone with the desire could learn to fly. He held himself personally responsible for everyone's success, and his flying experience enabled him to see the little mistakes we needed to correct. He had us spend a lot of time doing hangar flying — as important as actual flying. I believed my sole purpose was to live, breathe, and think flying, and hangar flying was an essential part of the process.

Our planes were primary trainers: PT-13s and PT-17s. The PT-13 had a

Jacobs engine, and the PT-17 had a Lycoming engine. That was the major difference. The airframes were Stearman. They could take all the strain a cadet could inflict in normal operations.

It was not long until we began to have more washouts. Those who did not really want to fly were the ones who failed. Anyone could learn to fly, but not in the time we were allotted. The Army had reasons for the rules we had to follow, so we did it the Army way, or we didn't do it at all.

I was fortunate to be among the first 10 percent to solo. That was the high point: taking off alone, flying the pattern, and landing. It was a sense of accomplishment that nothing else could equal. It was all up to the individual. I was happy and proud.

The instructor normally flew in the back and used a gosport to communicate with the student. It was a funnel-like apparatus attached to tubes that ran to the student's ears. It insured perfect one-way conversation. There was no way a student could interfere with what the instructor wanted to say. The instructor also was adept at using the stick to get the student's attention. He could crack the student between the knees with the stick without affecting the flight of the aircraft.

We were about halfway through Primary training when the first accident occurred. A cadet was approaching too high and landed on a plane below him that also was landing. The propeller from the top plane cut the parachute off the back of the cadet below. It then cut out the instrument panel in front of him. It missed the cadet, and they all landed with no one seriously hurt.

Within an hour of that mishap, another cadet taxied into a line of planes where cadets were starting the engines. He lost control, added power, and hit more airplanes, producing our first fatality.

That day began a series of washouts. We didn't know who left voluntarily or who had been forced out. But we did know that many had asked for voluntary reassignment.

Even with all of his experience, my instructor said he learned something on each flight. We knew we learned from him, but wondered what he could have learned from us. I have never met a more dedicated pilot than Orlo Watson. He thought of little other than flying. We all wanted to be like him.

Most of us believed we could see better than anyone else. We were flying one day at Puente, one of our auxiliary fields which was only a pasture that we used to shoot landings. I had made a couple of landings when Watson told me to go in and touch down in the same place.

I did, and he said, "Make a 'full-stop' landing, not just a 'touch-and-go.'" As I taxied back, he said, "Stop." He got out, walked into the field, bent down, and picked up something.

When the training session was over, I asked, "What did you pick up?"

He pulled out a fountain pen and said, "I saw it on a previous landing."

Chapter 2

Now, that was vision.

We also were told why airplanes were feminine in gender: They were not dependable and might take off at any time in a new direction! And, as with a woman, the pilot had to stay ahead of the plane, or it would start flying him. Airplanes and women, we were told, were beautiful to watch, but they made a man earn the right to be in command. And thus — the feminine designation.

Some cadets took check rides with Army pilots, but I made my last flight with my own instructor. We did some air work and then shot landings. I thought I had never done better. When we finished the third landing, Orlo said, "You haven't learned much. Take a good look at the wind tee." It showed a crosswind from the right.

On the next landing, I decided I would do it right. I set up a slight wing-low crab (dropped the wing going into the wind, kicking the nose a little into it as well). I was proud of myself. I went in, but made a poor landing, bouncing and weaving. Watson said, "Look at the wind sock." It was hanging limply in the air.

I was never cocky after that. I considered it the most important lesson I could have learned in flying. I knew I had to consider all indicators and make a decision based on all available evidence.

I looked upon completion of Primary as my introduction into the fraternity reserved for those who fly — such a fraternity as sea captains might have had years ago. We were just beginning to pay our dues in the fraternity of fliers. I was proud to join this group. After all, 21 of the 26 who started out on that train from Seattle to Santa Ana had already washed out.

Chapter 3

We left Ontario and the orange groves with reluctance. Our Basic training flying school was at War Eagle Field, 10 miles north of Lancaster, California. Although Lancaster was not far in miles, in climate we moved from the lush California Valley to the Mojave Desert. That was a long way.

The farmland north of Lancaster faded into desert as we approached the base. The nights were typical of all deserts — cold. So the school issued fleece-lined parkas for night and cross-country flying.

We lived in dormitory rooms, a couple dozen cadets in each bay. After the two-man rooms at Ontario, this communal living was a step backwards. But we soon learned that flying the BT-13 Vultee Vibrator would more than make up for the living quarters.

When we arrived, we felt the pressure to progress quickly as pilots were urgently needed in both the Pacific and European Theaters. We were doing much of the ground school on our own, because we flew so much that we missed classes. Flying went on night and day.

The BT-13 had a good Pratt and Whitney engine and plywood sections in the fuselage. The BT-15 trainer had a Wright engine. The Wright engine loaded up easily and required constant watching.

The basic trainer was a low-wing monoplane with fixed landing gear. The plane had basic instruments and could perform instrument flight. It had an altitude indicator, rate-of-climb gauge, altimeter, airspeed indicator, compass indicator, and engine instrumentation. It had two-way radio communication and airways navigation equipment. Instrument flying would prove to be a challenge.

I drew a contract instructor who was younger than I. Here the teaching approach differed; the instructors had a different attitude. They gave us credit for having some flying competence, but we would learn night, cross-country, and instrument flying. It was a big step up in level of difficulty.

A Lockheed test pilot, Don Hoover, came to Lancaster with a P-38 Lightning, one of the best fighter aircraft of World War II. He flew an exhibition, making half of the flight on one engine. It was a pitch for an accelerated course, skipping the rest of Basic and Advanced. Volunteers would go to a special check-out program in the P-38.

I didn't volunteer for the P-38 program, though I considered it, as did many others. But I believed I needed all the training I could get. I made that decision using my head, not my heart. I loved the looks of the P-38, and Hoover's exhibition was very impressive as he did aerobatics with one engine feathered. But I had sense enough to know I was not Don Hoover.

One of my New York friends took the bait. I heard later that he was killed in North Africa right after his arrival there.

The difference in age caused a problem between my instructor and me. On one occasion we were doing air work after shooting landings. He took control in the back, peeled off, and flew extremely low over his girlfriend's house. She came out to wave and watch us go by.

On one pass, we were headed for a Joshua tree that he apparently did not see. I could see it from the front and was afraid we were going to hit it. I considered taking over, but taking the control of a plane away from an instructor was not a wise action, tree or no tree. So, we hit the tree, cutting off a limb four to six inches in diameter and four feet long. As we flew back toward the base, the engine began making a horrible noise, and we couldn't keep the prop pitch at a constant rpm. My instructor turned the controls over to me as we approached the field. When we were on the runway and had slowed enough, he climbed out onto the wing, dropped off, and went into our Squadron Operations room.

I parked the airplane and wrote up what had happened to the plane. We could hardly deny flying too low since that was the only way we could have hit a big Joshua tree. And we could hardly deny hitting one with four feet of it stuck under the cowling!

I knew that my instructor was angry. Perhaps he had expected me to prevent the accident. I thought about it over the years and concluded that I should have yelled something to him or taken control.

For my next flying period, the morning one that ran from 0800 to 1200, I had a posting to take a check ride with the Squadron Commander. From 0800 until 1100, I just sat around, waiting for the call to fly. I was nervous because a poor flight could result in my elimination. I can't say I remained detached, because it was the first time elimination could affect me.

The Squadron Commander came in at 1100, smiled, and said, "Why don't you go to early lunch? I don't need to ride with you." I left like a shot. This told me everything I needed to hear. From then on, however, I only spoke to my instructor when absolutely necessary. He always acted with fairness, so I could not complain.

One beautiful day I was on a solo flight just practicing. I did some instrument work and had just started aerobatics when the engine quit. Before I could react, it restarted. I could not produce a malfunction. The power was normal, and all temperatures were in the green. I stopped aerobatics and did more instrument work.

I flew back to base, and did not experience any malfunction while landing. I ran the plane up and checked. I could find nothing wrong, nor could I make a malfunction appear. There was nothing I could write up.

That evening, the other class was doing night flying. Our group went to the theater to watch a movie, and when we came out, we heard that there had been a fatal crash.

The incident of my engine cutting out came to mind. I went down the next morning to check, and sure enough, the plane that crashed was the one I had flown. I looked up my instructor, and we talked to the Squadron Commander who checked it out. There seemed to be no connection between the engine malfunction I had experienced and the crash.

Because no problem could be found with the aircraft, the board decided the pilot had become disoriented. I knew they were telling me what they believed, but I could not fully accept their conclusion. I felt that there was a chance that the young man had died from a plane malfunction. Had I written up my experience, would it have saved him?

My Squadron Commander called me. He had me read the accident report which clearly stated that the cadet was doing unauthorized aerobatics at night, became disoriented, and crashed. I appreciated the Commander's effort to resolve my doubts.

From that incident on, I exercised more care in writing up malfunctions, realizing that if pilots did not tell the maintenance people when they experienced abnormalities, possible problems might go unchecked.

I was on a cross-country a few days later, when halfway back to the base, I noticed the airspeed was dropping. The manifold pressure was low, and the rpm gauge was oscillating. I had ample altitude, and the engine was still running, so I did not declare an emergency. It was a relief when I looked out on the horizon and saw home base. I made a long descent at minimal power and had no apparent problems. I called for landing and got clearance to call on

Chapter 3

final.

Everything appeared to be under control. I proceeded to turn on final, when the cadet ahead of me had problems with his landing, so the tower told me to go around. But when I tried to add power to my engine for the go-around, I could not get full power, only black smoke and a lot of engine banging. The good old Wright had loaded up, and my low power on the long descent had increased the problem.

What a fool I was. I should have declared an emergency as I approached the field. I finally did so and told the tower not to stop my landing if I made it around. I held as much altitude as I could, but it was not more than 50 feet. With the grace of God, I made it, and landed on the runway where the engine died. I had to be towed to the parking area. I was learning!

One day we flew all aircraft over to the Marine Corps base at Mojave and returned on buses. In the meantime, it had clouded over, and we found out what rain was like in the desert. It came down in torrents, though it did not rain long, and the dry lakes became seas. I was happy to be in the upper bunk as we had several inches of water in the barracks. We flew the birds home the following day and returned to our normal routine.

The weather was ideal for my first night flight. We flew from an auxiliary field. It was one of the dry lakes set up with portable lights. The Shuttle has since landed on that bit of real estate many times.

The airspace over the auxiliary field consisted of four zones. We would fly at an assigned altitude in the zone prescribed. The planes flew at 1,000-foot levels, maintaining separation from each other. I drew upper zone four.

The night was clear, and there was a full moon. We could see for miles. The cadets assigned to the upper zone were the first to take off and climb to their altitude. Then came those assigned to the next lower level in order. This procedure prevented anyone from flying through traffic.

I could read the instruments by the moonlight and did not need the fluorescent lights. When my hour was up, I started listening for the radio call to go down and land. I heard nothing and began to suspect I had a radio problem. I called but got no answer. I watched for the green flashing light that would direct me to go in and land, but I saw no lights.

At the two-hour point, I still had received no call, nor had I seen any green flashing lights. I decided to go on down and call on the radio from closer to Ground Control. I heard cadets screaming at me to get out of their zones, so I climbed back to my own. I flew around until it was time for the period to end, then landed and taxied in.

Our Squadron Commander climbed into the back seat of my aircraft. He told me to take us home. I could not contact Control, but did see the light signals. I took off and returned to home base. I could not contact the tower, and once again had to get a green light to land. The Squadron Commander tried the radio and got no one.

We got out of the airplane, and as we were walking in he said, "It's a lucky break for you making good landings." I accomplished my night flying for Basic on one flight. In addition, I passed a night check ride. A bad landing could have put me on the "wash rack."

The blind confidence I had had leaving Primary disappeared. I was learning that fate and I controlled my destiny. I was starting to recognize my own ability and to have confidence in the system and the rules I was learning. I was receiving a concentrated dose of dedication, discipline, and certainly development, the "3 Ds" my father had taught me. That night I lay in my bunk and thought of my father and all he had done to prepare me for life. I felt very close to him at that moment.

We were then ready for the Advanced course that would complete our flying training. The mode of transportation to Advanced was the good old railroad. We traveled through the farmlands of southeastern California, crossed the Arizona desert, and stopped in Phoenix, Tucson, and on to the mining area of Douglas.

Long before we arrived, we could see the smelter stack at Bixby, Arizona, belching smoke into the clear blue sky. We didn't appreciate it at the time, but that stack and smoke plume would save the lives of many cadets who would become lost on cross-country flights.

Douglas, Arizona, was not much of a city, but we were not going to be in town much anyway. We could all feel the pressure of the training, accelerated so that we could enter the war.

At the time, the United States was not doing very well in any area. The Navy had pulled a big carrier victory over the Japanese at Midway, and the Army in the Pacific was moving north from New Guinea taking some territory. But the Germans were pushing the British all over in North Africa. Our invasion had gone well, but once locked in combat we were outclassed. America needed experience to go on the offensive. For the first time, the winner was going to have to have control of the air over the combat zone.

None of this really meant much to us as Aviation Cadets. I know now, however, that unless you have been in battle, you cannot comprehend the requirements for war. I doubted I would reach combat before the war ended, but I was getting very anxious for my training to be over.

Chapter 4

The cadets received little information on the war. There were always many rumors, and we did hear some news on the radio. We went to meals, slept, talked, and dreamed of flying. The Army provided no activities or news. There was nothing from outside resources, and we had no place to go. We were aware the war was not going well for the Allies. But just how bad it was, we didn't know.

We flew over west Texas most of the time. In the Wink and Marfa areas, gas burn-off fires made it difficult to follow the light line. We flew the radio range, the light line, or did pilotage. The light line had rotating beacons every 10 miles, and the backs of the beacons blinked out a letter in Morse code.

There was a saying: "When undertaking hazardous routes, keep directions by good methods." Each light blinked a different letter. We could determine our location by referring to the map and reading the code letters. When leaving a major city the first letter would be w, then u, h, r, k, d, b, g, and m. If we had not reached the next major city, the system began with the letter w all over again.

There were emergency landing strips along the light line where the beacons blinked a green Morse code letter. We became proficient in reading those letters.

We were flying AT-17s and AT-9s. The AT-17 was nicknamed the "bamboo bomber" because it was a skeleton covered with fabric. The AT-9 was an all-metal, twin-engine bird and was considered hot for that era. It did almost everything at 120 miles per hour. It took off, climbed, and let down at that speed. It cruised at 160 miles per hour, and for the time, that was fast.

The instructors were not there to teach the basics of stick and rudder. We already knew that. We were to get a lot of training in cross-country, instruments, night flying, and formation. We received a quick check-out and began training to become proficient. We were readying ourselves for combat aircraft. A "gung-ho" spirit took over.

My good fortune held. I drew one of the few non-military instructors. He had had a lot of flying time and reminded me of my Primary instructor. He had flown a lot with his hero, Milo Burcham, who held the world's record for upside-down flight.

Each instructor picked those cadets allowed to check out in the AT-9. I was one of two in my group selected and soon found out that it was fun to fly a bird that was more challenging than the bamboo bomber.

A friend of mine from Seattle volunteered to fly one Saturday with a fellow student who had fallen behind. They were to meet an instructor and fly formation. They were circling and waiting for the instructor when the fabric tore off one of the wings of their plane. The cadets had no chance to get out, and both died in the crash. This was the first close friend of mine to be killed.

The Army was not looking for reasons to wash us out of Advanced training; they were honing our skills for war. After we became proficient, we flew cross-country flights without navigational aids. We made night landings at blacked-out fields. One of the instructors landed ahead of us and set up a portable light to guide us in. Then we called his plane on the ground for instructions. For many it would be the only communication system used in combat.

At this point, we could still wash out, but if we did it would be because of an ineptitude for combat flying. We all knew we would need the skills they were teaching us.

The Army went far past legal limits to make our training meet combat needs. It later stopped this type of training — the hair-raising, full-stop landings under the hood — blindfold landings — in the AT-9, because they were too dangerous.

The instructors showed a lot of nerve. Each had five cadets assigned to him. In my group, we had a person from Kansas who wanted to fly more than anyone else, but he got airsick on every flight. He carried a paper bag in the cockpit and used it to hide his sickness. He kept losing weight, but he would not give up. I admired him.

I, too, wanted to fly, but could not have put up with sickness on every flight. I later heard he stayed on as an instructor. He was a good pilot.

One Sunday, near the end of Advanced, we visited Agua Prieta, Mexico. It

Chapter 4

was situated along the border and reeked of poverty. We were treated okay, although we represented a lifestyle that the people knew was not available to them. Their poverty made me sad. But I could do nothing about it, so I wanted to stay away from it.

Back at school, my instructor had to recommend assignments for all the students. "You can have any assignment you want. You can, if you wish, stay here as an instructor," he told me.

The offer was tempting because I missed my family, but it would not be particularly good for my career. My goal was still to fly the B-17 Flying Fortress bomber in combat.

He said, "You can have fighters or light bombers." I decided to stick with the B-17, even though those going to B-17 first-pilot training would not get leave after graduation. I hated myself for passing up an opportunity to see my family, but I chose B-17 first-pilot's school.

I had been living on my pay of $75 a month, increased by my poker winnings. Dad sent my family money to live on. I would be making more than $200 a month, including allowances, as a Second Lieutenant — a big increase. I felt rich, because it was the most I had ever made. We would finally be financially independent again.

My wife was the one who had had to put up with a lot. She had the boys to raise alone, not knowing whether or not I would return from the war. She had to balance the budget and keep up family morale. She never complained once or questioned any decision I made. Jeri and the other wives in the same situation were the real unsung heroes of the war. They had no promotions, received no medals, and had little fun. It was a tough time for them.

I had signed up for flying in March 1942, and it was May 1943. Our second son, Gordon Burriss, was more than a year old. I had not seen my family for a year. But we were not alone in that separation; many people were going through similar experiences.

When my mother-in-law's uncle in California died and left each member of the family a small settlement, it was enough for Mabel to purchase a small house. The family was much more comfortable there. She had a job in a defense industry, packing weapons and other war supplies in Cosmolene to prevent rust during shipment. We felt it was patriotic to do something for defense, and it also helped to keep up morale.

When our orders came, everyone going to B-17 school, as expected, was to go there directly without leave. A surprise came for those going to other heavy bomber outfits — they were not getting leave either; they would be copilots. Others, however, got ten days' delay en route reporting to their new assignments.

Our movement once again was by train. We left the morning after graduation for Hobbs, New Mexico. On the way, we made a short stop in Piote,

Texas. Two pilots dropped off there to train as B-17 copilots.

The little town of Piote resembled a scene from an old Western movie. The terrain was flat, and it was hot and dusty. The only visible vegetation was the sagebrush dotting the landscape. The town consisted of some dilapidated buildings needing paint. The sagging buildings had seen better days.

The only sign of life was an old Indian sitting on a box on the station platform. He looked as if he had not moved in days and did not intend to. A hound dog lay alongside the building, trying to take advantage of the shade. The elderly station agent walked as though the movement caused him pain.

A hawk circled overhead, looking for dinner. It looked more accustomed to failure than success. Down the tracks from the depot were loading pens for cattle and horses. A small Army bus sat in front of the depot, the driver not in view.

I was traveling with Bill Ross, a friend all through flying school. He was also going to Hobbs. He was from Clark's Summit near Scranton, Pennsylvania, and the desert was a new experience for him.

We looked up the street. It would not have surprised us if a gunfight had erupted in one of the saloons or at the corral. We hoped that Hobbs, New Mexico, would have more to offer.

I realized then that no matter how bad I had it, someone else had it worse. I had been feeling sorry for myself at the time, but Piote broke the spell, and I began seeing events in a more positive light.

We finally arrived in Hobbs. It was larger than Piote, and the surroundings seemed better. But it wouldn't matter, because the only other time we saw the town was when we left after completing school.

The school officials greeted us upon arrival. We checked in and received our schedule which showed we were to go to the flight line that evening. There was no more of the cadet routine, such as marching to classes and Mess. We were Lieutenants now. We were pilots and wore silver wings. It was a new world, one in which we had responsibilities. We had each matured in flying school. We had shown dedication, discipline, and development.

We shared rooms again. There were no more daily inspections, but they had trained us well — we automatically set up the room just like we had as cadets and lined up our shoes under the bunks.

We had expected that the evening at the flight line would be just an orientation. It was a shock when we got there and met our instructor. He said, "All right, out to the bird. Pull the walk-around. I'll watch and correct. We still have time for four hours in the air."

The B-17 looked larger than our hangars back in Advanced training, but the walk-around went quickly. The instructor told me to get into the pilot's seat. The other student sat in the copilot's seat.

Our instructor swung in between us on a jump seat where he could reach everything. He had no intention of acting as a chauffeur.

We had been on the base less than eight hours, and we were about to fly a B-17. By taxi time, it was getting dark, and the four throttles were a handful. We received clearance onto the runway and took off. The power those four engines put out was a new, wonderful experience for me. I was glad to be there and knew I was going to be a first-rate pilot.

That first flight went beautifully. The instructor had me do instrument work for two hours, and then the other student did his two. We came in and landed, and thus ended our first flight in the B-17.

We flew at least four hours each day and attended ground school classes at least eight hours a day. Our main ground school instructor was a man no one would forget. He had a nickname: "Full Boost Weider." He was a solidly built man, medium height, with a handlebar mustache. He kept track of everything we did on the flight line. He had no hesitation about using actual events to illustrate points; he was trying to educate us. If we were going to come out of the war alive, we had to know all there was to know about the planes we flew.

He stressed that we would do much of our own maintenance. His favorite saying was, "You keep the fans turning, Sarge. I'll watch the railroad track." That basically was his way to fly and stay alive — by keeping an eye on the railroads and where they led.

If he thought a student was dozing, that student was in trouble. He would have the student stand up, explain some system on the B-17, and draw it out in detail. It had better be right!

Our first order of business was to complete 54 hours of instrument flying. That had to take place before check-out for solo flying. With two students per instructor, that meant we had 108 hours in the airplane before solo flying. During this time we were taking off and landing under instructor supervision. He taught us the type of pattern for the landing we would make. He wanted a minimum-sized pattern, a low approach, and the wheels down on the runway numbers.

He wanted every landing to be perfect. He emphasized that in combat we would have to land 55 airplanes in a minimum amount of time, sometimes with wounded on board, sometimes low on fuel. Other planes might have intense damage; many would have to land quickly or crash. In just four weeks we were checking out in the bird for solo work. There was a big push on to get us to combat.

Our class had a Captain who had been flying for one of the commercial airlines, and we knew by the grapevine that he was having problems. Our instructor told us the Captain was unwilling to make small patterns and land on the numbers. The military way of flying was not the only way — and it may not be the greatest way. But it was the method the Army demanded. Because the Captain was not willing to fly the Army way, and there was no time to mess with nonconformists, he was quickly transferred.

In tactical units, all tasks are coordinated so that, even with personnel turnover, each new man automatically fits into the existing pattern. As inexperienced cadets, we had no problem doing it that way, because we knew nothing else. However, it was not easy for those who had flown before entering the Army. Those pilots had to learn the Army system and forget their old practices. Many could not or would not change.

There is no margin for error in flying. Ground school taught us what we needed to know about the B-17 and its systems, not just well, but thoroughly. Our lives and the lives of our crews would depend on that knowledge. The nation's survival depended on it, as well.

On one night flight, cumulonimbus clouds reached up 50,000 to 60,000 feet. I speculated that we would stay in close and practice landings. We took off, and I was in the pilot's seat. My instructor had chosen to ride in the copilot's seat with my partner in back.

Once we were in the air, he asked if I had ever flown in hail.

I said, "No."

"There's no time like the present," he said. He told me to fly under the heavy build-up of clouds while he studied their coloration.

About that same time, we heard a call from base for all aircraft to land, and then they started calling planes in by number. My instructor said, "Don't answer them, or we have no choice but to land."

He had found what he was looking for and pointed to a particularly large build-up of clouds with a greenish tinge. He directed me to climb and enter just over the roll cloud. It protruded from the bottom front in the direction the cloud was moving. It was dark by then, but I could see the cloud and proceeded as he had directed.

What we flew into was worse than anything I could have imagined or that he might have expected. The hail was thick and at least golf ball-sized. Our windshield was shattered by a million cracks. I could see dents in the leading edges of the wings. We hit a down draft, and the rate of climb pegged on the descent side.

The instructor shouted, "Hold the attitude at all costs. Don't chase the rate of climb. Keep the airspeed off the red lines, both high and low. Hold to the general heading to insure penetration."

I was scared, not only of the present and real danger, but of the consequences. Just then we hit an updraft, almost equal to the downdraft. The hail disappeared, and conditions began to calm down. My instructor explained the benefits of our experience. He pointed out that we were over flat terrain. In that part of the plains, we could let down to 50 feet and not worry about hitting any hills. He directed me to let down, get on the range, and find our base.

There was only one little problem. Static prevented me from tuning the

Chapter 4 23

radio compass. When I thought I had tuned in the station, the needle oscillated so much it was useless.

The instructor said, "Don't worry. Cruise around underneath until we find a town. Then follow the railroad through town, and read the sign on the depot."

I had misgivings, but it was his call. We saw a runway dead ahead. My instructor said, "There's the base. Drop the gear, and make a straight-in approach." In the meantime, he called the tower. He told them we had been out of radio contact and requested a straight-in approach to runway 27.

I dropped the gear and proceeded in. We were ready to flare out when we saw telephone poles along the runway! I poured on the coal and started to climb out. My instructor said, "It's Lovington, New Mexico!" The main street almost had become a landing strip for our B-17.

From there the instructor knew the heading home, so we went on in. We pretended to land out of the "straight-in" original course as we had radioed earlier.

My instructor wisely recommended we say nothing about the flight. He said, "I'll handle all reporting." We were most happy to do just that.

I will always remember the look on the other student's face during the lightning flashes. He looked as if he might never leave the ground again if he could just get back in one piece.

This experience might have been what saved my life in later flying. I had learned what hail could do. I knew that many of the big hailstorms would be too much for any aircraft. And I sure knew some techniques to follow if I ever got into such a predicament again. I also knew my instructor was doing what he wanted to do most — *teach*. He succeeded! When we finished school, that airplane was still getting repairs to its skin.

My instructor had been a pillar of strength throughout the whole episode. He had complete confidence in the B-17 to take anything that came its way. He wanted us to know exactly what severe weather was all about. Conditions were worse up there than anyone could have expected. We learned to avoid thunderstorms at any cost.

Nothing in flying impressed me like that incident. I would not have taken anything in the world for the experience. But I would not choose to repeat it. The instructor had stretched the rules a country mile, and I sincerely appreciated his having done it. I found out I could remain calm under stress. It was a good trait to have. It was more of the "3 Ds" my dad had taught me. The school brass might have questioned the instructor's actions and the damage to the airplane, but I applauded what he did and his motive for doing it.

Chapter 5

Planes at the Hobbs, New Mexico, base had logged more than 100,000 flying hours without an accident. Everyone was proud of the record. Our class finished all of the dual-instrument flying. I had completed my checkouts for solo flight and was rightfully proud of my accomplishments as well.

The school brass decided to rotate one student from each instructor to a different one to measure instructor standardization. I stayed with my own, however, and was joined by a student from another.

On our flight, my instructor gave the new arrival the pilot's seat first and took the copilot's position. I drew the jump seat. We flew to one of the auxiliary fields to practice landings.

The student took off, flew to an auxiliary field, and made the approach. My instructor turned to me and said, "This is the type of low approach I have been trying to get you to make."

It looked too low to me. There was a barbed wire fence about 100 feet short of the runway. I knew we were going to hit it.

My instructor was busy telling me how good the approach was and did not look out the front windshield. Suddenly we felt a lurch as the landing gear caught the fence. The plane bounced up onto the end of the runway, and I saw a fence post go through the right wing flap.

The instructor stopped his lecture and began to pay attention to what was

Chapter 5

happening. I could tell we had lost our brakes. We rolled the length of the runway.

The instructor told the student to unlock the tail wheel and turn off. We were moving at a good clip, and would run off the end of the runway if we didn't turn.

When the student pilot unlocked the tail wheel, we made a ground loop and ended up spinning on the end of the runway. The instructor took over the controls and gunned the inside engines to make a larger circle. As a result, we ran off the runway. He stopped the engines, and we got out to check the damage. The main problem had come when the fence wrapped around the landing-gear strut. It broke the hydraulic line to the brakes, and all of the fluid had drained out. There was also minor damage to the flaps from the fence posts flying up and hitting them. There was nothing to prevent us from fixing the broken brake line and flying home, so my instructor cranked up the radio and informed the base.

Two other B-17s had followed us to the auxiliary field. They were circling, waiting to begin shooting landings. The first to try a landing came in on the approach. It was off to the side of the runway. It touched down, tried to take off again, but was caught in sagebrush and sand and couldn't get up enough speed for takeoff. The crew came to a fence, power line, and county road and had to ground loop so as not to cause severe damage to the aircraft and possible injuries to crew members. They had cut off the power pole with the wing. They shut down, walked around, and looked at the damage, which was minimal. And even though it was more than we had experienced, it would be considered minor.

We stood and watched the third plane. It had a picture-perfect approach. The pilot made an excellent touchdown on the runway. But then one wing got lower and lower as the left gear slowly went up into the wheel well. About halfway down the runway, the wing tip touched the ground, and then the number-one engine propeller. It did a slow turn-off, into the sagebrush and sand.

The school's perfect record had been broken with three accidents in a row. You had to witness this to believe it! Not a person sustained injury, and the damage to aircraft was slight, so the pain of what had happened diminished knowing there were no injuries to personnel and only minor damage to the planes.

We were called to testify before the Accident Board, however. It was my first experience in front of any kind of board, and I wondered if I could be in trouble. Yes, I decided, I could; but I fortunately was not.

I heard my instructor give his testimony. I didn't like it. He said, "I saw we were too low. I tried to add power, but the student had frozen at the controls. I couldn't overpower him in time."

Graduation class 43-E from Hobbs, New Mexico, in the B-17 first pilot course.

The truth was that he had not seen that we were too low until we had hit the fence.

I came to believe that the school authorities chose this story to meet several needs. Headquarters could forgive a student, but not an instructor. After all, students are in the learning process and will make mistakes. I was sure my instructor said what he did to cut the losses for the school and all concerned. When accidents happen, personnel sometimes play musical chairs — everyone changes jobs, which presents the illusion that corrective action has been taken. It's done from Headquarters up the chain of command.

I didn't approve of telling anything other than the whole truth, but this was my rude awakening to the "real world." I still believed my instructor was a superior flier, and if I ever got into trouble, there was no one I would prefer having with me in the cockpit.

The balance of the school was a piece of cake. Time passed quickly. Then the big day came. Graduation and first-pilot qualification were rewards indeed.

I had orders to go to Moses Lake, Washington, for B-17 combat-crew training. It had been a year since I had seen my family, and Moses Lake was

Chapter 5　　　　　　　　　　　　　　　　　　　　　　　　　　　　27

very close to my home. Surely I would get leave. I sent word to my wife that she and the boys could go over to my parents' place in Kennewick. It was closer to Moses Lake than Seattle.

Our movement was on the good old railroad again. We headed north and stopped in Las Vegas, New Mexico. We were told to go uptown and get something to eat because the train would not have a diner on the leg to Denver. They assured us we had plenty of time.

We ate and returned, only to find that the train was pulling out early and leaving behind many passengers. We all hollered at the train conductor and someone must have heard us, as the train backed up for several miles. It was the only time I ever saw a train back into a depot that it had just left.

For troop movements, the railroad seemed to provide the oldest and most run-down equipment possible. The military had to accept this, whereas paying customers did not. Although it was not a particularly pleasant trip, we got into Denver at four in the morning. We remained there most of the day, and most everyone went uptown.

We resumed the journey that evening; as we went through Wallula Gap, I could almost see my parents' farm. A real temptation existed to drop off, walk over the bridge, and go home!

The train arrived in Spokane. We would go on to Moses Lake the next morning, so we had the night in town. My wife's college roommate, Phyllis, lived there. We also knew her husband, Jack. He was in the Army, awaiting release because of his size. He had been a professional football player and was too large for Army gear.

I called Phyllis. She came out, picked me up at the depot, and we did the town. It was good to see her and to hear about Jack. They had married before Jeri and I had. We laughed a lot about the "old days." Odd how a couple of years passing becomes the "old days" for the young!

We left the next morning for Moses Lake where we checked in with our Squadron. We learned that there were twice as many first pilots as they needed, but no copilots.

I went to our Squadron Administration Section. I could see no reason not to be allowed a few days' leave to see my family. But then I didn't know the workings of the Army. It did not run on logic or reason, but on rules issued by Headquarters.

My request for leave was rejected outright. In fact, they laughed at me for making the request. I went to see the Squadron Commander, but he refused to help in any way. It seems the Air Force had a policy preventing anyone going on leave while in crew training status. To grant an individual leave could interrupt training. There were no exceptions.

Parked on the ramp were B-17s that had flown the night before. An enlisted man going past one of them kicked one of the guns protruding from a ball turret. That started it firing, and the turret made a 360-degree circle, firing all the time. The 50-caliber bullets ventilated the walls of nearby buildings. Luckily, no personnel were hit or wounded, although some of the aircraft parked on the flight line were damaged. That incident would delay training even more.

Several days passed, and we did nothing but wander around. We learned that the Officers Club was outside the main gate and across the road. Anyone could take off from the Club and go anywhere he wanted if he had transportation.

Bill Ross, my friend from Pennsylvania, and I talked it over. We felt cheated at not being given leave from Advanced as had the others. Tomorrow was Friday, and we didn't appear on any schedule. The next week's schedule was out, and we were not on that either. Why not go over the hill? We could get someone to call us if we were needed. Chances are we wouldn't even be missed, so Bill planned to go to Spokane for some rest and relaxation. We arranged for him to get a call from a friend on base if he had to return quickly, and then he would then call me. I was going home to see my family.

At that point in my life, a year away from my family was an eternity. So I

Chapter 5

arranged for Dad and Jeri to pick me up outside the Club, and I went AWOL for the first and only time. It was worth it!

I got a call from Bill about midweek. He said, "We have orders. We leave tonight." Our friend had done a good job for us. He had cleared post for us and had our new orders. We were going to Gowan Field in Boise, Idaho, for B-24 Liberator training. Dad and Jeri drove me back to Moses Lake. It had been wonderful to see her and the boys.

B-17 jockeys considered the B-24 just a crate used to ship B-17s. But a B-24 was not an airplane that just anyone could fly, and we felt we would be lucky if we lived long enough to get into combat. The B-24 had a Davis wing, with a little different airfoil that couldn't be flown at a low speed. Many were crashing for a variety of reasons. I wasn't pleased about my assignment, but could only follow orders. The only good thing about it was that Bill Ross would be going to Gowan with me. We had become good friends.

We were traveling by train again. Eight of us were being transferred to Gowan Field. Our rail car was so old it had wicker seats and carbide lamps. There was an old potbellied stove in the rear of the car.

The woman who ran the telegraph at the depot had boarded with us. Her shift was over, and she was going as far as the next station. Bill and I found a seat about midway in the car and were trying to get some sleep. I could hear her talking to a couple of the other pilots. She said, "We'll be going on the siding here. A large Navy Special has priority over everything else."

I dozed off and awoke later as the train started to move out onto the main line. Then the woman shouted, "My God, we must stay on the siding until the Navy Special passes."

I felt the train going into reverse. I raised up and looked out the back of the car directly into a large headlight.

I grabbed Bill, pushed him along ahead of me, and we reached the front of the car. There was a *whoosh* as the Navy Special shot past; amazingly it had not hit our car. We felt bumps and shudders, and then all was quiet. We looked out in all directions but could see nothing in the darkness, so we climbed down.

A Negro porter came out of a mass of wreckage. He had a flashlight and was saying, "Oh, my God, they are all dead." He didn't stop, but continued up the track, repeating the same thing over and over. We didn't see him again.

We tried to climb into the car next to us but couldn't. Planes flying out of the Moses Lake and Ephrata bases saw the wreck and flew low over the trains with landing lights turned on. That was the extent of the light we had.

Medical teams came from both Moses Lake and Ephrata. They had to cross the fields in the darkness to get to us. The Navy train was carrying recruits and had a doctor on board with some medical supplies. We organized into groups to help; some walked up the track and found members of the trains' crews, including the engineers of both.

Our train had pulled out onto the main line, then had tried to get back, but could not; and the crew had jumped. The crew of the Navy Special had also jumped when they saw that they could not avoid impact. The two engines collided and peeled off into the fields on either side of the track.

Many on the Navy train were injured as it telescoped inside itself. The doctor assigned some of us to crawl through the wreckage. When we found a body, we injected morphine into an arm or leg. We found out later there were 45 dead and several times that number injured.

We found one sailor jammed between the sides of two cars. He was in a space no more than four inches across. Bones were sticking out of one arm. Steel car sides had bent both legs into an arc. He did not complain about his arm, but he did complain about the pain in his legs. An officer used a fire extinguisher to douse the flames when the blankets covering him caught fire. They had been ignited by the torch being used to cut into the side of the train. At five in the morning he finally was free; only then did he pass out. The wreck had occurred near midnight.

When first light of day came, we could see that there were few still alive in the cars that had telescoped together. It became apparent that we had shot morphine into many arms and legs that were no longer attached to bodies.

There were enough medics from the bases by morning, and there was nothing more we could do. We took stock of ourselves; we were a dirty, bloody mess. I thanked God for that medical officer who was on the Navy train.

A new train was sent out to take us into Spokane. We asked a railroad employee if we could shower and change clothing, but he said, "No deal!" — there was no time; we had to leave on the new train or not at all.

We then left Spokane on a train not scheduled to arrive in Boise until early the next morning. It had been a long time since our last meal, so we tried to get into the diner, but the manager said it would be too upsetting for the other passengers. Of course, that made us angry, and I told him we would file a complaint just as soon as we arrived at our base in Idaho.

The manager finally agreed to let us eat in the diner after all of the other passengers had finished. That was gratitude! I doubted anyone would have complained about us and thought the manager of the diner was just being arbitrary.

I was concerned that news of the train wreck would hit the papers and cause Jeri to worry, so when we got to Boise I called her. She had not heard about it, however; the government had managed to keep the news away from the media. And because she already had too much to worry about, I didn't tell her. In 1943 the American public didn't hear much good news; more bad news certainly wasn't needed.

We arrived at Gowan Field at Boise about eight in the morning, reported

Chapter 5

what had happened, and asked for a day off. The officer on duty said, "No problem. We'll see you tomorrow." Now that was the way fliers should operate — reasonable decisions made by and for flying people. I loved them!

Boise turned out to be a pretty city with ideal flying weather. The quarters were excellent. We bought a Mess card good for four meals a day, including midnight chow. The meals at Gowan were the finest I had in the service. I enjoyed them more than any others I would eat for years. The room and Mess reduced my disappointment at having to leave the B-17s.

Chapter 6

The officers in charge at Gowan Field had all survived a tour of combat. Some were survivors from the 19th Bombardment Group stationed in the Pacific when Japan had hit Pearl Harbor. Others were survivors from the original Ploesti raid in Europe. All were veterans who had paid their dues. They knew the score and were operating the base for the benefit of the trainees, not to please some Headquarters staff.

We were assigned to crews and started crew check-out. The instructors wanted to find out if we could handle the B-24, and if so, to get to flying.

The B-24 Liberator surprised me. The B-17 Flying Fortress was an aileron plane, whereas the B-24 was a rudder ship. The B-24 Pratt and Whitney engines were superior to the B-17's Wright engines.

My check-out pilot was an All-American football player from the Carolinas. He covered the points I needed to know quickly and turned me loose. I learned that when flown correctly, the Liberator would take good care of me. I liked the plane. Its ball turret was inferior to the turret in the B-17; but it had superior engines, and the nose turret beat the B-17 chin turret.

There were other pros and cons as well. The Liberator would not fly as high as the Flying Fortress, but it had superior performance below 20,000 feet. Pilots normally sacrificed airspeed for altitude. However, in the B-24, airspeed loss would not save altitude. An empty B-17 could keep going on two engines, but the B-24 needed three to fly and hold altitude.

Chapter 6

Our instructor hated any type of headgear, so he wore none. He liked short sleeves, so he had the sleeves of his summer uniform shirts cut off. His All-American and Combat Veteran status seemed to entitle him to get by with violating such regulations. After several flights with us, he said, "I know better places to be enjoying myself than flying around the sky with you guys." We saw little of him after that.

The base Commander apparently felt much the same way, and the place reflected it. His policy was simple — accomplish the job and forget the "Mickey Mouse" stuff. That was all right; we were flying and enjoying it.

One day after a flight, we went over to Operations and watched a B-24 take off. When it was airborne, it began to belch heavy black smoke from one engine. It was in a nose-high attitude, then dropped off on one wing, crashing into the ground.

Before I had been checked out, the crash would have bothered me. Now it did not. I was sorry to see someone get killed, but it didn't devastate me as it might have before.

My crew was sharp. The bombardier was a character. I often would find him reading Plato. He believed the bomb tables were wrong and used his own. I accepted his disregard for procedures because his results were consistently superior. I didn't know what made him tick, but I liked the results of his ticking. We had made a dozen flights, and I enjoyed flying the B-24 with this crew; it was interesting. We would soon be ready for combat.

One Saturday morning we reported to the skeet range. We had spent Friday night in the Club celebrating, so I was not in good shape. I drew the high house to fire birds. I was setting them up and talking to a friend who was emphasizing a point, with his hand sticking in the high house. The man firing swung his gun around and shot into the house.

I was watching my friend's hand as it got hit, splattering blood on the walls. I helped him into the ambulance and accompanied him to the base hospital. The doctor finished with him and said he would be fine. Then he turned to me and said, "Now, let's take care of you."

I looked at my shoulder and realized that it had taken a good bit of the shot as well. My shirt and shoulder were a mess, but I had felt nothing. The doctor inspected my shoulder and said, "We can do either of two procedures. I can cut into the shoulder and dig out the shot, or I can simply treat it to prevent infection. The pellets will work themselves out." The latter sounded better to me, so he put medicine on and applied a bandage to the wounded area. He was right — for years afterward, shot worked its way out, one at a time. He could have done a lot of damage if he had dug all of it out of my shoulder. I was hit twice by gunfire, and neither time in combat. I no longer liked skeet shooting or rabbit drives!

While at Gowan, my roommate, Bill Ross, and I decided one day to go uptown and hit the state liquor store. Idaho had bottle laws, which meant that hard liquor had to come from one. We put our wallets on our beds while we showered, then dressed and started walking toward the bus stop. A worker leaving the base offered us a ride and dropped us at the store.

We went inside, signed for our cards, and picked out a few bottles. At the check-out stand, we realized that our wallets were empty. Apparently while we were showering, someone had stolen our money. The free ride to town had kept us from finding out at the bus stop on base. We had to return the bottles to their racks and hitch a ride back to base. We reported what had happened; and fortunately we still had our Mess passes and could eat until payday.

The worst individual any outfit could have is a barracks thief. The Military Police had their eye on a suspect, an officer who had been losing heavily at poker. We hoped the Army would catch the guilty person and cashier him.

Shortly afterwards, four first pilots, including Bill Ross and I, received orders sending us to Sioux City, Iowa. It irritated and disturbed my crew that we were to be separated, so I went to Operations to see if there was any chance of getting the orders changed to let me stay with them.

At Operations I was told, "These orders come from too high up. No one on this base can do anything." The entire crew tried but had no luck. It felt good to have a crew that felt so strongly about flying with me. They were good men, and we all had gotten along with no problems. The bombardier took it hardest, however. He packed up and left, saying, "If I can't fly with you, I'm not going to fly." I hope for his sake he came back.

We arrived in Sioux City after another journey by train. I hadn't slept much; I spent my time looking out the back, watching for a headlight.

There were two flight groups at Sioux City, both B-24 outfits getting ready to go overseas. I was assigned to the 448th Bomb Group, Heavy. The other was the 446th, which had a pilot named Jimmy Stewart, the famous actor and a Captain in the Army. I saw him in the Officers Club but did not meet him personally. Those who did said he was a regular fellow who remained unimpressed by his fame.

The officers of each crew shared a room. Mine were already on board and in quarters, so I went to meet them. I would meet the enlisted men later. My copilot was a young officer fresh from flying school. His home was Charleston, South Carolina, and he seemed to be a very solid type, someone I could accept. The bombardier was a neat person from Peoria, Illinois. He was immaculate in dress and presumably a talented officer. He made a favorable first impression. The navigator, a former instructor at Navigation School, was from Chicago, Illinois. I would have to reserve final judgment on them until we flew together, but I was happy with the officers on my new crew.

Then I met with the enlisted men. The engineer, the ranking man, was from Texas. The radio operator was half Indian and came from North Carolina, the

Chapter 6

ball turret gunner from Pennsylvania. The waist gunners were from California and New York City, and the tail turret gunner was from Oklahoma. They ranged in rank from Buck Sergeant to Technical Sergeant.

We all went to Squadron Operations to check our schedule and learned that the new aircraft Commanders were first to fly with the Squadron Operations Officer for check-out. We assembled the next day in Operations and went out to a plane. It had been loaded with all sorts of items to build up the weight, including a large push fire extinguisher. Practice bombs and work stands added more bulk.

The Operations Officer told me to take the pilot's seat. He climbed into the copilot's side, and we started the bird. With the loose load, I didn't dare do anything that would cause weight to shift. I was extra careful as I wanted to get off the plane when my turn flying ended.

We took off and flew the pattern; I made one of my better landings. The Operations Officer told me to take it around again; I did and made a better-than-normal landing a second time.

As we started on the third trip, the Operations Officer looked over and said, "I haven't made a landing this month. I need one. I'll make the next landing from the copilot's seat." I felt relief. I didn't have to fly any more on the check. He did alright, although his landing was not as good as mine had been. He taxied in, dropped me off, and told me to get my crew ready to start training early the next day. That completed my check-out.

Before I dropped off to sleep that night, I thought about my crew. The engineer seemed to be a good man who had a lot of experience and knowledge. He was older and had lived a rough life on the Texas plains, but I thought his face showed the signs of a man who had used a lot of alcohol. I would have to keep him from that. The others were young boys who could be molded into a good crew.

As for the officers, the bombardier was obviously a good man and should give me no cause for worry. The copilot was young, but he would do. The big question mark was the navigator. Why had he left an instructor's job? I would have to find out by trial and error. I had to know everything I could about my crew. We were going into combat together, and we each had to do our job for all of us to survive. But I felt these guys would do it.

I learned that the rest of the 448th Bomb Group had already been together for awhile; they had all had phase training in Wendover, Utah. This stop was the final preparation for overseas deployment. Each Group had to have 72 crews to qualify as fully manned. Ours was short, as there had been two recent crashes that had killed some crew members.

I found out that when we received our flyaway aircraft, the Group would have only 15 planes per Squadron. Three crews in each Squadron would go with the ground personnel on the ship. I vowed not to be one of them!

Most crews had finished training and were just staying current and enjoying life. Everyone was eager to get in on the action. We were still flying each day and some nights, trying to accomplish all of the required training. I was pushing hard because I wanted us to fly overseas. I had had my fill of trains and did not want to try boat travel.

In the push to accomplish all of our training, we flew in bad weather and took chances. I had to make on-the-spot judgments and pray they turned out right.

One Friday night, our flight was to be up the Missouri River to the Cheyenne Agency for gunnery. The weather was not good, and the forecast was for it to get worse. We went to the aircraft and checked the forms. The last flight had been for one hour; the paperwork showed that the number two engine had taken 32 gallons of oil. However, it wasn't possible for one engine to consume that much oil on a one-hour flight; there had to be a problem, perhaps a broken oil line.

I looked up the man who had serviced the airplane and asked if he had really put in 32 gallons.

He said, "Yes, Sir. I added 32 gallons of oil."

I informed the crew chief who told me he would handle the airplane; I was just to check the servicing, not give opinions on engines.

I looked up the line chief and showed the forms to him. He said that the bird only took 32 quarts and that the person on the service truck couldn't tell a quart from a gallon. I asked if the aircraft was checked, and he said it had been. Then I asked him point-blank if anyone had removed the cowling. He became angry, so I thought I would probably not receive a true picture from him.

I checked in with my crew. They had found that the guns were dirty and rusty, and doubted that they were operable. So I had the crew pull the guns and take them into our Squadron Operations Office. We laid them on a table, along with the aircraft forms.

I put in a call to the Colonel in charge of Group Operations; I located him at the Club. He was not happy to be bothered on a Friday night, but he came at once, probably intending to reprimand the upstart of a Second Lieutenant silly enough to call him during Happy Hour.

The Colonel was breathing fire when he arrived in Operations. He said, "What's going on here? Are you afraid to fly at night in a little weather?"

I showed him the forms that said the engine had been serviced with 32 gallons of oil after a one-hour flight. Then we pointed out the condition of the guns.

He called the line chief and ordered him to pull the cowling from the number two engine. When the cowling came off, there was a broken oil line in the rocker box on one of the cylinders. By then the weather had deteriorated, and a cold rain had begun. Ice would hit us just a thousand feet up. The Colonel put in a call to the armament section. They had only one person on duty; he told the Colonel that the shop had shut down for the weekend and would not open until Monday morning. The Colonel was furious.

I told him if they put a new line on the number two engine, we would complete the mission. He said firmly, "No way!" He told us to scrub the flight; we would begin flying when the planes were ready. Then he ordered a roundup of all personnel and told them to start fixing every aircraft. Everyone on the base was to work around the clock, continuing until all needed maintenance was done on all planes. There was more activity on that flight line than we had ever seen before. The fur was flying, and I knew that I would not be popular in many places; but so be it. I had to let the top brass know what was happening.

I had not backed down, and we had made our point. I found out the next day that inspection of the engine had resulted in a complete engine change. We had won that round, but the time had come to perform. We went back to flying day and night.

In a few days, I looked up the line chief, and we had a long talk. I knew that everything would not always be perfect. But I did expect the proper servicing of all items affecting flight safety to be beyond reproach. I wanted only the truth. I told him in plain terms that he could count on flying right along with us the next time such a problem arose. From then on, he personally checked in with me whenever I flew.

The line chief had worked in the Pratt and Whitney engine factory in Connecticut and was able to teach me a lot about the engines that was not in the book. He also gave me a special screwdriver that I could use to adjust the boost for the engines while in flight, which I carried throughout the war. We parted as friends, both having understood how our relationship was going to be.

As I had received ten days pre-combat leave, I checked the airlines for flights home. But even with military priority, I risked getting bumped, so I chose to go by train once again.

By the second day, I began to feel as if I were a stockholder in the railroad! But it would be wonderful to see the boys and my wife, even if just for a few days. Jeri worried about where I might be going, and I was curious, too.

When I returned to base, I found the selection for flyaway planes posted — we were going to fly! But there was still one big hurdle for the Group to pass — the "Palm Inspection." A team would arrive, go over the records, fly with our crew, and decide whether or not we were ready.

The Group Commander feared that the inspectors would find out we had not accomplished all of our training. So Operations scheduled us for our 2,000-mile cross-country training flight. This would mean that we would not be there to be checked by the inspectors. The long flight gave me a welcome opportunity to study the navigator, about whom I still had reservations.

We used celestial navigation during much of the trip. In the B-24, I could look down between the rudder pedals and see into the nose where the navigator sat. During the flight, I noticed that he would shake his head in doubt, even though he made positive statements. If I could see his head, I would know whether he really believed what he said.

The radio operator could get us fixes using the HF (high frequency) radio. I also had radio aids available, and we would cross-check the positions given to us.

After the flight I talked to the navigator about his behavior. He said in navigation school he had been taught never to let a pilot think he was unsure, even when he had doubts. Throughout our service together, I never felt I could rely on what he said.

Landing after our cross-country flight, we learned that we had passed inspection and would receive the flyaway airplanes within a week. The next day, several aircraft arrived, including mine. That was a day of much excitement as I signed for an aircraft, including all of the equipment, worth $250,000. It was a B-24 "H" model, the latest at the time. We went over it with a fine-toothed comb and found one defective bomb-bay door. There was nothing we could do but cannibalize a door from one of the old E-types on base. The paint didn't match, and it stayed that way; but we loved that bird!

We could fly as much as we wanted to check out the equipment. The only thing we found was a problem with the autopilot; but reporting it would have delayed our departure. Since we wanted to fly it by hand anyway, I didn't mention it.

I was still getting the feel for the B-24H when, on the following day, we loaded it with supplies, parts, and our own personal gear. It was a full load. We were to fly to Herington, Kansas, for yet another inspection, and thus we stayed for a day. We were placed under some restrictions when we arrived. No one could make a phone call. I had to fly an instrument check with an inspector, and although I passed, I did not feel like I had flown well. Several personnel were assigned to ride along to perform maintenance long before our ground party caught up to us. We found a minor fuel leak in one of the engines, so I contacted the line chief and asked for his opinion. He didn't think it was serious, but that it was something we should watch.

We had no idea where we would be going from Herington. But we were in the first wave, and I wanted to stay there. Some of the enlisted men began to speculate, based on the work they were doing on the airplanes. They didn't think our destination was the South Pacific; they thought that the work on our planes suggested we would be in cold weather.

Events began to add up — it would not be the northern route after all. We were pleased, as no one liked ice, snow, or the North Atlantic in the late fall. The next day we flew to West Palm Beach, Florida. Once on the ground, we went under lock and key again. We could not make phone calls or have contact with anyone outside of our Group.

We reported to Operations the next morning to plan the next leg. We would be on our way soon. That night as I lay in my bunk I realized fully that the stateside days of developing dedication, discipline, and development, and the training were over. I knew we were not through learning, but from then on it would be performance that counted. We must do everything right. Dead men would have no need for learning or development.

I was aware of the weight of my responsibility. I had a crew of nine other people who were putting their lives in my hands, so I had to measure up. My folks had done right by me and so had my instructors. I believed I could handle the job ahead. Then I thought about my wife and the boys who had the most to lose. It would indeed be a "sporty course."

Chapter 7

Morning brought a beautiful fall day in West Palm Beach. This was the day we had waited for throughout all of our training — the day we would find out where we would be flying combat. Maybe England, maybe the Pacific, or maybe Italy would be our destination. Today would tell the tale.

One fact we did know. Today we would leave the United States for what could be a long time. In fact, we might never come back. That was a very sobering thought.

I went to the Mess and ate, having no idea what I had for breakfast. Never in my life had so much been flowing through my mind at one time. The major realization was that training was over, and now it was up to me. I had a crew who depended on me to make all the right decisions. There would be no one I could turn to. From this time on our lives depended on the decisions I would make.

I remembered when my instructor in Advanced had asked me what I wanted to fly and I said bombers. Now, looking at those innocent young faces of my crew, I wondered if I should have said, "I want to fly fighters." Then only my own life would be at stake. Having all those boys depending on me made me feel older and quite serious.

After breakfast, it was off to Operations to plan the flight. Where to, we knew not. In Operations they told us to plan and file for a flight to what is now Ramey Field in Puerto Rico. That did little to show where we would be going

Chapter 7

for combat, but we did our planning.

The base appointed each copilot to be Finance Officer. Ours signed for $2,000 in gold-backed bills. We would be flying over countries without military agreements with the United States, so the money was to be used if we landed or crashed in some neutral or uncooperative nation to pay for labor, fuel, or parts.

Each aircraft Commander went to a room and signed for a sealed envelope. On the outside, printed in bold letters, were instructions to open the envelope only when we were past a given coordinate. We would learn our destination at that time.

We were about halfway to Puerto Rico when we reached the designated coordinates. I tore open the envelope and learned that we were to join the 8th Air Force at Station 146 near Seething, England.

We were happy to be going to England. We knew it was the hot spot of the world for combat flying, and we would be going up against the infamous German Luftwaffe. During the trip, we were to remain overnight in Georgetown, British Guyana. Then we were to fly on to Belem, then Natal, Brazil. From there we would fly across the ocean to Dakar, Africa, north to Marrakech, French Morocco, and on to Newquay, England.

The field in Puerto Rico was a garden spot resting on a plateau. A cliff in front of the Officers Club dropped straight down about 500 feet to the ocean. We could not have found a more beautiful setting. We sat outside in the lounge chairs, looking out over the ocean and sipping frozen daiquiris. If this was the way to combat, lead me on. It was a fun night, and all we talked about was going to "jolly old England."

I saw South America for the first time when we landed at the airfield in Georgetown, British Guyana. The small field looked like it was carved out of the jungle around it, which was so thick that from above it appeared to be a flat surface. A closer look revealed that the mat of jungle growth extended upward 200 feet from the ground, a thick green mass.

We learned that Tom Harmon, the All-American football player from Michigan, had crashed in that jungle in his B-25 shortly before we had arrived. He was the only survivor. From our vantage point, it did not look possible for anyone to have survived a crash in that tangled mess.

We landed, taxied to a remote area, and began what would become the daily practice of setting off a DDT bomb in the plane to rid it of beetles, flying insects, and other vermin hitching a ride with us.

As soon as we had parked, an army of young boys arrived. Initially they begged, then launched into a pitch to sell us melons. When this didn't attract any takers, they tried to trade shirts with us. That failed, too, so they tried to peddle their sisters. The Military Police arrived and ran them off.

We were quartered in open barracks with only a roof overhead. It was extremely humid, and the base had nothing of any interest to us. We longed to be back in Puerto Rico on the balcony in front of the Officers Club, sipping those daiquiris. It would be a long time before any of us would see luxury again.

I was awakened at 0600 the next morning and told that we were to take off at 0800 for Belem. I looked at the torrential rain outside and said, "I'm going back to sleep." But then I decided that we would not have been awakened if the orders had not been genuine, so I got everyone up. By 0630 the rain had stopped, as if someone had turned off a faucet. One of the permanent party personnel said it rained like that every day. I knew I had no desire to stay there.

The takeoff run was longer than usual. It shook me to be racing down the last bit of runway gazing into that green jungle ahead. I needed at least a hundred feet more altitude. I was afraid of crashing into that green mess, but we made it with a good bit to spare.

Our flight path kept us south of the northern ocean (the Spanish Main). I looked down into the never-changing jungle all day long. Now and then we crossed a river running to the north, but no bare ground was visible. There was only solid jungle as far as the eye could see.

We passed French Guyana and its famous, or infamous, Devil's Island, surrounded by shark-infested waters. Looking down into the jungle below, it was easy to see why no one could escape from the prison on that island where some of the worst criminals spent their last years.

Our flight plan was to fly straight to Belem. The jungle made me decide to fly a landfall on the coast. We would cross the Amazon and Oronoco Rivers, fly downriver a short distance, and find Belem.

Nothing had prepared me for the size of the Amazon River. It was immense. I lost sight of land. Cattle grazed everywhere on the large island, owned by the Rockefeller family, that was at the mouth of the river. Our briefing had specified not to fly low over the cattle if we flew over the island. Texas ranches were little dirt farms compared with this spread.

Belem proved to be an interesting base. It had a large post exchange, and we arrived early enough to shop. There were boots for sale that were poor copies of Justin Ropers, but size six was the only ones they had. The smaller fellows could get boots, but those of us with big feet were out of luck. I found a Swiss Tissot watch I loved, which I bought and mailed to Jeri; she wore it for years.

The Officers Club at Belem was much like those stateside. And we were assigned to rooms, not an open bay. The jungle appeared less thick on this side of the Amazon River, less threatening. Perhaps I had just become used to it.

The following day we flew to Natal on the coast. Like Belem, Natal was humid and uninviting. But it was a lot better than Georgetown. At briefing we were told to keep records of our fuel consumption. If we were not satisfied with it, we could make a flight to Rio and back to check it out. We could not

Chapter 7

land at Rio, though. I would like to have flown down over Rio to see it, but I was afraid I would drop out of the front ranks and I wanted to stay in the first wave.

We kept track of how much fuel we used on each leg. We were the first B-24 H-model aircraft to cross the ocean and had greater fuel capacity than previous models. Consequently, we could skip landing at Ascension Island. We made our flight plan and discovered we would fall 75 miles short of Dakar at the rate we were burning fuel.

I had read an article by Charles Lindbergh, telling about flying P-38s in the South Pacific. By using a higher manifold setting and lower rpm, his gas consumption was lowered. His method had become standard, subsequently providing a greater range for P-38s. I knew that we had our center of gravity too far aft for good fuel consumption. I also had heard that cracking the flaps just a mite would keep the plane on the step with lower power settings.

We had the next day free, so we shifted our load, moving a lot of the baggage to the nose. I looked up the line chief, the former Pratt and Whitney man, and asked him what power settings would use the least fuel and still be safe for the engines. He recommended 34 inches of manifold pressure with 1,650 rpm.

He said, "Keep your eye on the cylinder head temperature; keep everything in the green. Stay alert for any vibration in the propellers or engines. If you have any, raise or lower the rpm, until you find a setting where vibration stops."

We took off for Africa at 2000 hours flying at 8,000 feet. We had four extra people flying with us to handle our maintenance until the ground party arrived by ship. The weather people had said that the most favorable tailwinds for crossing would be at 14,000 feet. I told the crew and passengers that we could handle that altitude even though we didn't have enough oxygen masks for everyone. Some individuals could put oxygen on if they needed it. None did.

When we were about 800 miles out of Dakar, I was already receiving it on the radio compass (nicknamed Bird Dog because it pointed to the station) and was homing in. We planned for a landfall to the north. If we missed to the south, we were still a long way from land.

We flew over Dakar and got clearance to land on the pierced-steel-planking (PSP) runway. When we had landed and parked in hard stands, we had 1,250 of the 2,790 gallons we had started with. Lindbergh's technique, along with the others I tried, had worked — no one else had nearly that much fuel remaining. The first thing we did was spend 15 minutes spraying the plane with DDT.

The base Commander assigned a native to guard each aircraft. We were given a password to use if we had to go back there for some reason. Each guard was over six feet tall and had muscles on his muscles! A football coach would have gone wild over these guys. The native men wore turbans and had a white cloth around their waists. They each carried a dangerous-looking machete which was at least three feet long and resembled an Iowa corn knife. Each also had at least one knife attached to a belt around his waist, similar to an American hunting knife, decorated with stones, along with a rifle. Their skin was ebony, made blacker by the contrast with their white robes. They had very large eyes. I was sure they were fine fellows, but I didn't want to find out whether or not they could speak English or recognize the password. There was nothing that could have made me go to the plane during the night. I'd leave it to the guard to handle everything until morning.

It had been a long flight, hand-flying the bird. We were tired, so we hit the pad early. Each bed had a screen of green or tan netting covering it. We were cautioned to get into bed, zip up the netting, and be sure all openings remained closed. Disease-carrying mosquitoes were the main problem.

The next morning we headed for Marrakech, going north from Dakar and across the Sahara Desert. We had been advised at the briefing to fly with dust covers installed because sand in the air would damage our engines. Someone knew what they were talking about. The sand was so thick I could see nothing below, a real contrast from the green jungles of South America.

The winds were higher than predicted; there was red-brown sand up to 14,000 feet. We flew a bit higher to protect the engines, even though we had installed the dust covers.

As we flew north, the Atlas Mountains remained hidden in a cloud bank. I called the navigator and asked the height of the mountains. According to the him, they reached from 3,500 to 4,500 feet.

When we came to the clouds, I thought we could descend safely because the sand would no longer be a problem. We set up a steady descent, entered the clouds, and were down to 10,000 feet when we broke out into a valley with snow-capped peaks towering all around us. I couldn't believe what I was seeing. I was on the way down to 5,000 feet, which should still have been above the mountains. I had the navigator pass up the map, then realized that the elevations were in meters, not feet! That was the last time I took anyone's word for anything. I hit full power. We could probably go through the valley we were in, but I wanted to get on top.

From then on, everyone I flew with would have to prove everything to me. "Show me" became my middle name.

It was not long before the mountains dropped down into the plain. The clouds ended, and we could see for miles. Marrakech lay on the valley floor, while to the north was more desert.

One of the gunners called, "Fighters at two o'clock in the sun." No one had mentioned fighters at our briefing. I didn't know their country of origin or what their intentions were, but I didn't intend to wait around and find out. Setting up a slightly descending flight path, I left on plenty of power, letting the airspeed build. The fighters turned to follow us but were falling behind.

They never caught up. I liked that. We were in no shape to fire any guns — ours were empty.

When I could contact the tower at Marrakech, I asked about the fighters. I was told that they were a Free-French welcoming committee. When they landed, we went over to look at the planes. Someone had wrapped rope around the wheels because the tires had worn out. They were pathetic. It was no wonder they couldn't catch us.

After we had landed, we were assigned by crew to small buildings serving as barracks and told that we would be there until how we were to fly on to England was worked out. The Germans had been flying out and intercepting unarmed bombers going north to England, shooting many of them down.

While we had been at West Palm Beach, our bombardier and a couple of the gunners had found and signed for two 20mm cannons and ammunition. They thought we could mount them in the waist of our B-24. So that night we armed our plane. We were ready to go north to England as soon as Headquarters made the decision.

At Marrakech we ate from Mess kits at a field kitchen. The Free-French wanted us to scrape our leftover food into their tin cans, as apparently no one was taking care of them. When I looked at them, I knew we could not afford to lose the war.

The old huts we stayed in had previously been French Foreign Legion facilities. They contained cots and nothing else. Each of us had one blanket, not enough to keep a man warm down there near the Atlas Mountains where it got quite cold at night. By dusk we knew we needed heat, so we went on a search mission.

We located empty barrels and found one with the top removed. We appropriated it and found enough old wooden boxes to make a fire. We were warmer, but we almost died from the smoke. We could not clear it out of the room and decided to find somewhere else to spend the evening.

We found a truck driver who would drop us off in town at the Mammonia Hotel where we sat and drank out of dirty glasses. When we were full of the local red wine, we caught a ride back to the base and slept in our sheepskin-lined flying gear. Between the wine and the gear, we slept well. There would be no more fires in the barrel.

The next day we roamed around, looking at the local sights and the people. Most of the natives wore desert clothes — turbans and robes — that they could shed in a hurry to produce a wicked-looking knife instantly. They were feisty people. Most had something to sell, including knives, trinkets, and pictures of nude women. We were carrying our .45s in shoulder holsters, so we were not a bit afraid. Maybe we should have been more cautious.

We went to town again the next day and walked into the old walled city. The local meat market was in an open square. Ground meat, hidden under a covering inches deep with flies, was piled atop a large flat stone which served as a showcase. We saw dogs lift their legs and urinate on the stone and the meat. We had planned to eat in town, but after looking at the "meat market," we decided we were not hungry. Apparently the natives had built up a resistance to the filth.

A group of local toughs started to accost us just as a Military Police jeep came around the corner. The MPs explained that it was permissible to visit the town, but that the old city was "off limits" to American personnel. They offered to drive us out, and we accepted their offer gratefully. They said there were not enough police in all of Africa to protect Americans venturing into the old city. There were miles of tunnels and passages known only to the natives. According to the MPs, it was an armed camp filled with degenerates of all types and descriptions.

I was happy to be out of there. The two crews who went to town had elected me to carry the money because I was the biggest. I had put it in my shoes and was walking around on $4,000 worth of gold-backed bills.

Marrakech had hacks for hire, pulled by old horses whose skin sagged and bones showed. We got one that evening and took a ride around the city. The driver offered to take us past the Sultan's Palace for a small fee; he said we would see the Sultan's Harem. We paid him, and he took us down an alley and behind a castle-like building. By that time, we had a pretty good idea of what the major landmarks were. We knew we were in an alley looking at the back of the Mammonia Hotel. We had a good laugh over that one!

We went into the hotel for wine and ran into some other crews. They told us that there was going to be a meeting about flying to England, so we returned to the base and found that all crew personnel were being rounded up. We learned that we were going to fly to England that very night. Once again, thoughts of war became real, personal, and very close.

Chapter 8

Our forces in England desperately needed replacement planes and crews. Headquarters had decided to change the course for flying to England, so we were to fly farther out over the Atlantic before turning north to make an approach to England from the west. Hopefully this would keep our bombers out of range of the German fighters. We armed the guns on our aircraft. The weather was bad; we would be flying in "the soup," so we should be hard for any Germans to spot.

The briefer offered us several options for our climb out of Marrakech. He recommended making a wide, circular climb to get over the mountains before going on course. But each crew would have its own choice. One plane, using the recommended procedure, hit the mountains losing all on board. Ironically our Weather Officer was on that plane.

It was a bad night, but nothing approaching the intensity of the thunderstorms we had flown in over New Mexico. It was recommended that we fly a little to the north before going west to avoid flying over Spanish Morocco. Although Morocco favored Germany, it had never interfered with any bombers passing over it. However, I didn't worry about Spanish Morocco in this weather. We flew a direct course to the point for the turn to the north.

We were in the clouds all night. It was not rough, just eerie. I knew there were other planes out there, and some could be the enemy. I had all our turrets manned.

We were approaching the point to turn east for the run to England when the first faint light of dawn came. I received an interphone call from the tail turret gunner. "Sir, a plane is following us!"

I said, "I'll turn 90 degrees to the east. See what it does."

He called back, "He turned right along with us. He's still following."

I made a series of turns and each time got the same report from the tail turret gunner. I decided the time had come for me to crawl back and take a look for myself. Sure enough, what I saw looked like a plane following us.

We flew with the HF antenna extended so that the radio operator could send position reports. It had an oblong iron ball on the end of it to keep it extended. In the faint light, we realized that what looked like a real plane was that ball. No wonder it followed us! The crew praised the tail turret gunner for doing his job. We all had a good laugh and then relaxed.

We made the turn east toward England. We were supposed to let down and fly just above the waves, landing at Newquay on the west coast. We descended and could see that the water about 50 feet below was rough. We were now in a climate that was cold, wet, and stormy. It was a marked contrast to the route we had traversed.

As we got closer to England, we began to fly over many small fishing boats. The men did not like having us come upon them. At first we thought it was fun, but then I realized it was no joke to them. The Germans had used them for target practice for years. I made turns to show them we were friendly and were not going to attack.

We were within range, but I could not pick up Newquay on the Bird Dog, nor could I raise the tower. Apparently we were having radio problems. I asked my radio operator to call on HF. Newquay answered the call and said, "Continue your approach, land on runway twenty-seven, and watch the green altus lamp blinking the okay. Ceiling is five hundred feet and visibility one-half mile. Do you read?"

It sounded to me like the approach would be a bit sticky, but it was just a normal day in England.

We flew over the field, saw the green light, and landed. We were still in the first wave. We had been in the air about 13 hours and were glad to have arrived. We wrote up a report about the radios and took off to find a place to stay.

We were put up in a hotel in town. It was a cold, gloomy day, and we soon learned that was normal weather.

We had our first experience that night with a blackout. In England they meant it when they said *blackout*. All of the windows were covered. The headlights on all vehicles had covers installed with a tiny slit which let just a bit of light through and hid the headlight from the view of aircraft overhead. Drivers blew their horns to clear intersections.

People carried flashlights they called "torches with number-ten batteries."

Chapter 8

Jack Swayze in England wearing a 50-mission crush hat.

During an alert, the flashlights remained off.

England had been at war for four years, so the people knew what war was all about — privation, suffering, death, and destruction. They had wondered if America would come to their aid. That shocked us. They had fought and won the battle for Britain, but America had not come. Oh, we had a Squadron of American volunteers there, but we had not been there as a nation. The British accepted America's delay, but the English people were happy to see our airmen now. They had seen much, lost many, and still faced the reality of war. They had no choice. The British talked about the war the same way Americans talked about baseball.

Our radios were still out the next day. I doubted anyone at the base could fix them, so I called and asked permission to make the trip without radios. I was told, "We will call instructions for you."

That evening we received a call from someone on base who said, "We have arranged for an American pilot to ride with you. He knows England and you can come tomorrow. He will fly copilot and aid with navigation."

The next day we flew across England to our base at Seething, 14 miles out of Norwich. We could see from the air that we were assigned to a brand-new base, not an old Royal Air Force facility.

Once on the ground, we found something that all wars have in abundance — mud. It was everywhere. The roads on base had not been completed. We had to travel on muddy trails.

The Squadron assigned us living areas, two crews in each Nissen hut. We shared ours with the Assistant Operations Officer and his crew. I was happy to have a direct pipeline to the "head shed." Our living area was a half-mile from the Officers Club and one mile from the Squadron area.

The land between was still being farmed by a local man whose family had worked it for countless generations. We learned that he lived on the base with his family. They had a cottage with a thatched roof and were hard-working people. They spoke a dialect — maybe British, but certainly not American. It was difficult to carry on a conversation with them.

They had a small boy, and it did not take long to become acquainted with him. He was eight years old in the fall of 1943, and his name was Ralph Waters. Because of King George, though, we called him Georgie. He was a favorite with the crews and came by to see us each day. He loved to get American gum and candy. We bought cigarettes, shaving items, and writing materials, along with a small ration of gum and candy when it was available at the exchange on base.

Georgie kept track of all crews and suffered with us when one was missing. To those of us with families, he was a link to home. He did all right because he was the only boy on base and had access to all personnel.

Our living area had a coal-burning stove with an overgrown radiant stovepipe for heat. Our ration of coke was only one small pail a week — enough to take the chill off once. In the middle of the living area was a smaller hut with a latrine and washroom. There was no hot water. A row of wash basins ran down the side of one wall. The waste water ran into a trough, through the wall, and onto the ground outside. There were tubs in the Club area — half a mile away — with hot water provided by the Mess.

We could send our washable clothing to the base laundry and our uniforms to the dry cleaners. But the uniforms always came back reeking with the odor of gasoline.

Some bases were fortunate enough to be equipped with American cots and bedding. We drew Royal Air Force gear — a steel cot, three "biscuits" for a mattress, and a gray blanket. To my knowledge, no one ever invented a method to prevent a man's rear from going down between the biscuits during the night.

The day after our arrival, we had flown our airplane to the Depot at Watton

Chapter 8

Jack Swayze (standing, second from left) with his crew for their first tour in 1943-1944.

The Group mission briefing room, Seething, England, 1943.

for theater changes. The armor plate around the pilot's and copilot's seats was replaced with plywood that was painted green. It looked the same as the armor plate had. But the armor plate had caused bullets and flak to ricochet and do more harm than good, so the Depot claimed. The plate was heavy, so removing it resulted in a greater altitude capability and range for our aircraft. Numerous changes were made — to radios and engines — to prepare us for the theater and the climate. Stoves were made with the armor plate removed from our airplanes. It kept the Depot people warm.

We loved to go to Watton because their Officers Mess had tablecloths. They had ice cream at meals, and the bar served drinks with real ice. I volunteered to fly all planes going to Watton, but so did everyone else.

Our base had one Officers Club for combat crews and one for non-flying personnel. Ours was a "jumping" place while theirs was staid and formal. The division caused problems. The non-flying Mess was usurping food earmarked for combat crews. Consequently, the gap widened and hostility arose between the groups. Those who led the "good life" on the ground looked down on the fliers. Those who flew combat missions resented the second-class treatment. After all, they were risking their lives every time they flew. The only way non-fliers would be hurt was to fall off a bar stool!

New crews were still arriving. Some brought animals and birds, including parrots, with them. But the parrots were dirty birds, and most escaped into the British countryside.

One crew brought a burro from Africa. He disliked the flight so much that he kicked a hole in the side of the airplane. After landing, they still could not control him; he eventually took off across the fields, kicking at everything he could find.

Another crew brought a well-behaved puppy. They had made an oxygen mask for him. He flew on missions with the crew. They said they believed God would care for the puppy and, in the process, care for them. They might have been right.

I was promoted to First Lieutenant at this time, assuring that the Crew Commander was the ranking officer — not the most flattering way to gain a promotion, but I accepted it.

We were flying daily missions toward the enemy coast to confuse them about the target for the real raid and to provide practice in flying formation. This "gravy train" life, however, did not last for long, as more new outfits kept arriving. Finally we had enough planes back from the Depot to fly a regular mission and the time had arrived to begin fighting. We took off for Bremen, Germany, on 16 December 1943, flying an 18-ship formation.

The characteristics of the B-24 in flight made it difficult to handle that formation. I was on the outside, the last box of three, low and left. I stalled on left turns while the high right fell behind, no matter how much power they

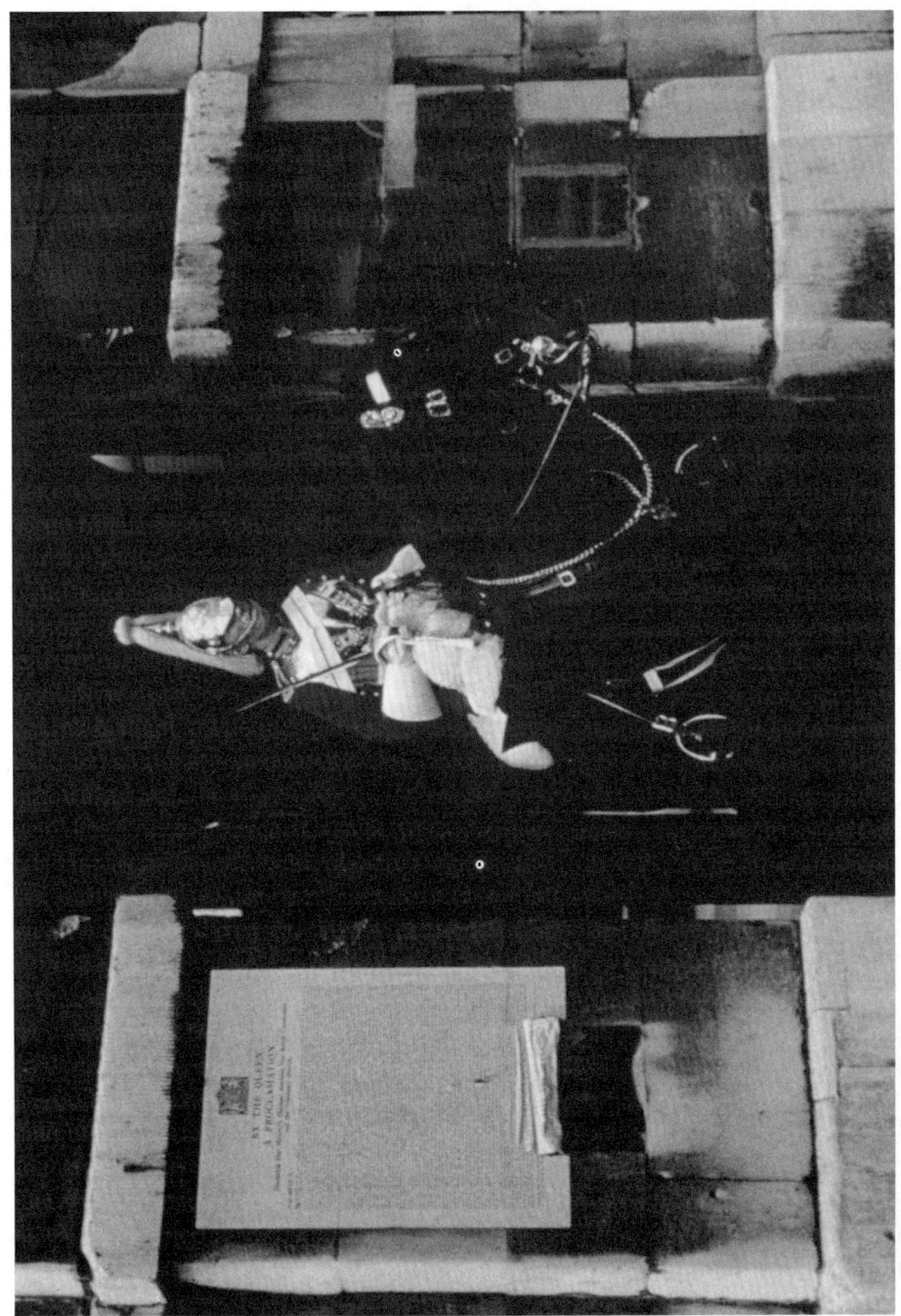

A guard and posted Proclamation by the Queen, London, 1944.

carried.

The weather was fine over England and the Channel. We crossed the coast, and our crew felt some concern as we entered German airspace for the first time. We were too green and ignorant to be afraid. We were just a bit north of one city and south of another. The flak came up from both cities but did not reach us. From a distance, it didn't impress us. It looked like a Fourth of July fireworks display.

When we came within the range of other guns, we began to take hits. We lost one plane, and the rest got some holes. We were short of the Initial Point (IP) when we received the recall. We couldn't make a visual run, so we returned to base.

Those of us who had flown in the low and high elements of the formation were unhappy with it. We couldn't make the turns and knew something had to change. Other Groups had watched us and had reported our poor formation performance. We fought to get mission credit, but to no avail. We still had not flown a combat mission.

Division made us fly practice missions to improve our formation capability. Flying practice rather than combat missions hurt morale. We all started looking at each other and being critical. But it was not the pilots' abilities that caused a problem. The B-24 simply could not fly an 18-ship formation successfully.

Our next attempt at a combat mission was on 30 December. The target was a chemical works in Ludwigshaven on the Rhine River, 50 miles east of Kaiserslautern. The mission went sour. We flew a poor formation, got hit by fighters, and later ran into flak. We lost six crews and received bad reports.

Squadrons held meetings. Commanders made threats. Finally we had our chance to explain that the B-24 should not use an 18-ship box. As a result, we changed to a 12-ship box. That allowed the three-ship low left to slide under the lead box of six on left turns. The high right could slide over the lead box. The reverse took place for right turns. We had a better chance to survive.

The operator of the ball turret in the B-24 had to lower it to use it and raise it for landing. That was a problem. Convair had designed and built the B-24. The company loved hydraulics and used them to do many things; the tradition continued after it became General Dynamics. Boeing had used servo motors for everything in the B-17. Hydraulic systems leaked and electric motors failed; both had problems in combat.

Soon we had the ball turrets removed, getting rid of 1,800 pounds and a weapon that frequently failed. In formation, the ships alongside could shoot at anyone coming up from below. I was sure that many stragglers had gone down because they had no protection underneath. We began to fly like we should.

Our Group flew to southern France on New Year's Eve. It was a long haul, and many did not make it home. Four had gone down over France. My friend,

A statue of President Abraham Lincoln in London, 1944.

Bill Ross, was one of them. He did not appear on any list of prisoners of war, nor did any of his crew. We assumed they had died.

All crews realized we were not on a picnic. This was serious business. We had to look to our knitting to have any chance of surviving.

Headquarters had diverted a B-17 Group to our base during bad weather from the 1st Air Division, stationed in the midlands to the south and west of our area. We were the 2nd Air Division, and all of our planes were B-24s. (The 3rd Air Division, flying B-24s, came later and eventually changed to B-17s.) The Germans were hitting us more with flak than with fighters. The B-17 was better in flak; it could fly higher and take more flak damage than the B-24. But the B-24 could handle fighters better and could out-perform the B-17 below 20,000 feet.

We went to chat with the diverted crews. They had started flying operations in mid-1942, so many had flown more than 20 missions. The most any of us had was three. We heard a lot of combat stories; many were probably untrue, but we learned a lot.

War in the air did not involve a German person against an American person. Crew did not face crew. Plane was not pitted against plane. Rather, confrontation was impersonal and directed "to whom it may concern." Luck was to be a big factor in who survived and who didn't.

I knew I had to fly with skill if we were to survive. No one would do it for me. We had already found out that war was not glamorous or glorious. It was Hades, pure and simple.

For the first few months, we didn't have electrical power to our huts. That meant getting up in the dark to fly and going to bed in the dark. And each crew had only one bicycle. That was ridiculous! How could four guys ride one bicycle? The bicycles soon became useless; most had flat tires or were stolen. If not, the mud did a job on them, messing up the bearings and the brakes.

As winter arrived, we found that the only way to sleep was to pile everything we owned on top of our blanket for warmth. We also learned that the more we drank, the better we slept. Occasionally Scotch was available, but mostly it was gin in juice. But when we drank a lot of beer, we couldn't make it through the night, and would have to run that quarter-mile to the latrine. It was an unpleasant occurrence anytime, but particularly in the middle of the night. After a latrine trip, I could never get warm again or back to sleep. I just lay there shivering. War was miserable. We were never comfortable.

The schedule, once posted, remained in effect until a crew flew a mission. If a mission was scrubbed, the crew stayed on schedule to fly. In the winter of 1943-1944, we had rotten weather in Europe and flew only a few raids. Our crew was on alert for more than 30 consecutive days.

We awoke each day between 0100 and 0200 for early breakfast. Then, we rode the six-by-six trucks to the briefing. Most of the time we went out to the planes and prepared for takeoff. Then would come the red flares fired from the tower, signaling "Mission Canceled."

The worst part of any mission was the briefing and waiting to take off. That was when we worried. Once we got started on the mission, we were too busy to worry.

Captain Black, the Assistant Operations Officer, and I had a discussion and agreed not to fly the same missions. That way if either of us got shot down, the one not flying would fly over the Channel to look for the ditched crew. It was our idea of additional protection. Most of the time, those missing did not make it to the Channel to ditch, but even so, we were happy with the arrangement.

Big changes took place early in 1944, not only in our aircraft but also in our formation. We were receiving B-24 J- and K-model aircraft. They were not the usual olive drab color, and they gave our performance a boost — literally. They had an electronically controlled boost, which made formation flying much easier. It was set by turning a knob to a number. Some came equipped with formation sticks, improving conditions for the lead pilot.

Most of our planes no longer came from Convair, but from Ford Motor Company's Willow Run Plant. They flew a few miles an hour faster than the planes built at the mother factory.

The fuel gauges in the B-24 were connected by pipes to glass tubes about one inch in diameter and a couple of feet in length. The tubes hooked to the back wall of the flight deck, and free flow from the main tanks allowed the fuel level to be seen, depicting the depth of fuel in the tanks. In combat, however, glass tubes filled with high-octane fuel shouldn't be in the cockpit, so the Depot capped off the lines. Thus, in flight, we could only guess at how much fuel remained. During pre-flight we used a stick to check the amount of fuel in each tank.

The B-17 had electric fuel gauges and could also gravity-feed the fuel from the outer wing "Tokyo" (auxiliary) tanks. The B-24 could not; fuel could only be transferred by pump, and there was only one way to tell whether the transfer pump was working. Your engineer had to crawl through the bomb bay to the waist. Then he had to go up over the bomb bay, reach up, and hold the tubes in his hands. If the tubes were throbbing, it was likely that the pump was working and gas was going into the main tanks.

In the B-24 we took off on the main fuel tanks and would fly at least one hour into a mission. Then we would run the transfer pump for an hour from the auxiliary tanks. We were by that time over enemy territory, and I would not allow my flight engineer to leave the top turret to walk and crawl back there when all he could find out was whether or not the hoses were throbbing. The predicament was absurd. If you found out that the fuel was not moving, nothing could be done about it. You were going to the target in any case as long as the bird would fly. Throughout the war, there was no change in this

Chapter 8

An unmarked B-24 joined our formation for a few minutes. It was probably a restored aircraft, flown by Germans to obtain and relay exact data to their defenses. The aircraft would not answer our radio calls. We did not shoot him down, however, because he could have been a stray — a friendly — but we could have. A few minutes later, he dropped out and disappeared into the undercast. His radar dome is clearly visible under the aircraft.

procedure for checking the fuel supply on a B-24.

Another combat problem was the system of gunnery taught at gunnery school; it was a complicated mess. It would have taken another budding Albert Einstein to work out the correct gun lead in combat. We learned from experience that we could use a very simple formula for setting the lead. We would take the clock location of the attacking planes and use one, two, or three rads (radical rings) as needed.

The rules called for arming the guns upon reaching altitude out over the Channel — but this was no good. On takeoff in the winter, slush was thrown up onto the guns, and they would freeze up when we climbed. And at altitude over the Channel, there was no way we could charge the guns. So we ignored the rules and charged the guns before we taxied. Then when we were on top, we fired them. That broke loose any collected ice.

The rules also called for rubbing only a very light coating of oil on the guns. We learned that if we dipped the guns completely in oil, our gun problems stopped.

We found out that the Germans were flying captured B-24s. They flew alongside our formations, relaying routes, exact altitudes, and other pertinent data, giving the German flak batteries a big advantage. Because of this, Bomber Command revised our unit markings to make detection of those captured aircraft easier and more definite.

In 1943 and early 1944, we were escorted by our own or British fighters only part of the way to the target. Then on the way back out of Germany, fighters picked us up again. The Germans knew this and waited for the escort to drop off before attacking the bombers.

Germany also added new 105mm and 120mm guns which were more accurate at higher altitudes. And by this time, both sides had also improved their radar capabilities.

The Germans almost put an end to the British bombers when more than 700 were lost in one night. We flew over the English Channel and the North Sea to locate downed British planes so that air/sea rescue units could pick up any survivors. All that my crew saw was one wheel floating in the sea.

On 11 January 1944, we flew to Meppen and Zundberg, Germany, sustaining a lot of flak damage. We also got hit by German fighters as soon as our escort turned back to refuel. Some of our oxygen lines and tanks took hits. We suffered until we could get to a lower altitude where we could breathe more comfortably. That proved to me the need to conserve oxygen. If we didn't, we could end up a casualty — just a statistic.

We flew to St. Pierre de Jongurer, France, on 14 January to hit a factory. Once again we got hit pretty hard by flak and fighters. I began to think I was not flying correctly. We had so many holes and so much damage. But how could we have had so much damage without anyone aboard being injured?

Chapter 8

A Group formation of aircraft above the clouds.

I knew someone was taking care of us! But how long could I depend on that someone if I did not shape up my flying? I believed it was my fault that we were taking so many hits. I must not have been flying well enough to protect us. I certainly no longer had to worry about the war ending before I had arrived; I had to worry about survival.

On one of those early missions, we came back with more than 3,000 holes in the plane. We found it hard to believe that all those bullets hit us and missed hitting anything critical enough to cause us to crash.

When attacked by fighters, we were supposed to fly close formation. Then all the formation's guns could hit the bandits. A loose formation was flown in flak, allowing individual evasive action. The exception was in barrage flak over major target areas. Then all anyone could do over the target was to fly the bomb run and pray.

But even in a loose formation, we had to be sure we did not let a spread condition develop. Any gap allowing German fighters to split us up created stragglers who might take hits from coordinated attacks by a swarm of fighters. Yet, I knew that when batteries on the ground locked onto a plane in formation, that plane had better take evasive action.

I tried to discuss my concerns with the staff, but they did not seem to understand what I was saying. Their priority was tight formation flying over Wing and Division Headquarters. This looked good for the ranking officers and visitors from the Pentagon. But it didn't always suit the needs of war.

Since most big cities had antiaircraft weapons that fired barrages into a box-like space covering the whole area with flak, we could tighten the pucker string, bore on in, and pray. Another thing we could do was to track flak. If a burst was about 200 yards in front, we did nothing. The next burst would be only 100 yards in front, and we would see the red or orange center. If we did not move then, the next burst would get us.

I learned to go into a continually increasing turn because the gunners could track us perfectly if I continued in a straight line. But in the banked turn, I learned that the bursts followed me into the turn. The increasing bank, however, kept me inside the bursts. Then I would turn back into the burst because they would not hit twice in the same place. Rather than starting a whole new problem to pick up our track, the gunners would pick another plane.

There were a lot of flying tricks that I learned to prolong our lives. I was reading a paperback Western about a gunfighter who was a genius at staying alive. He had rules, but the most important was to keep someone between him and the guy doing the shooting. It hit me hard because I knew I had not done that. I vowed to start flying better.

I also studied the German fighters. Many hung back, looking over the bomber stream. They wanted to live, too. If we were firing and another outfit

Chapter 8

was not, the fighters went after the easier pickings. This told me that our gunners must fire sooner. So we kept our turrets pointed at their fighters before they committed. All of our strategy and tricks would work if we flew smarter than the enemy.

Chapter 9

Many combat crews had spent or gambled the government funds they had received for emergencies en route from West Palm Beach. Until our ground party arrived, there was no one to accept the money. And there was plenty to do with cash, including dice games with thousands on the table, along with high-stakes poker and passes to London, which could be expensive.

Some crews got hit and went down with the money on them or hidden away in a place known only to them. We were dealing in English money in England. Americans spent English pounds like American dollars, even though one pound was the equivalent of $4.86 in American money.

When our ground party arrived, it was interesting to watch the crews try to recoup the missing money. The ground party wanted the money turned in for return to the United States government. In one instance, a copilot was in the same poker game as his Squadron Commander. The Lieutenant desperately needed the pot to replace the $2,000 advanced to his crew for emergencies.

The other players folded, and it came down to the Lieutenant and the Squadron Commander. The Commander knew the pot would give the Lieutenant the money he needed. He stalled, and the number of spectators grew. The Lieutenant was perspiring. His hands shook as he stared at his cards. He finally called. The Squadron Commander waited an agonizing ten minutes before showing his hand. He did not even have a pair. He had just wanted to

Chapter 9

make the Lieutenant sweat. After that hand, the Lieutenant swore off poker for life.

My navigator would not give up gambling. He gave me his money each payday and told me not to give it back to him. Then he would come to me that night, begging and demanding his money until I gave in. He often won and sent home a bundle.

On 29 January 1944, the weather finally took a turn for the better. The day dawned as clear as it ever got in England. When the curtain was pulled open at briefing, the target was Frankfurt.

Headquarters was trying a new bombing concept. The first Group over the target would drop general-purpose bombs on the factory area north of the marshaling yard. These demolition bombs would blow buildings apart. The next Group would drop incendiaries over the same area, setting it on fire. The third Group would drop delayed-action general-purpose bombs to prevent the Germans from fighting the fires. They were set to go off at intervals from 1 to 36 hours. Then the 8th Air Force would bomb Frankfurt again before the delayed-action bombs stopped exploding. This was an intense way to hit the enemy hard.

One of the worst problems experienced frequently by crews on missions was ruptured turbocharger seals. This was especially serious if the plane was deep over Germany. Loss of these seals would reduce manifold pressure, resulting in loss of high-altitude capability and eventual dropping out of the formation.

The pilot could check the seals in the aircraft forming area over England by yanking back on the throttles with high boost applied. This action would normally burst any seals that were weak or near failure. I did this check before a mission to Frankfurt. All the seals for all four engines burst, leaving no boost at all. Each Squadron maintained a spare airplane loaded and ready for immediate takeoff, so I chose to land, pick up the spare, take off on course, catch the Group, and complete the mission.

As we approached the French coast, we had not yet flown long enough to transfer fuel from the Tokyo tanks. We took some flak crossing the coast near Dieppe, but I didn't detect any serious damage to the aircraft.

When it was time to transfer fuel, we ran the pumps for the prescribed hour, assuming the fuel was being transferred. Then we caught up to the Group, got into formation, and reported in. We had no problems over the target, and bomb results were good.

On the way home, within sight of the Channel, one engine quit. I knew we were nearly out of useable fuel; I had to do something in a hurry. We were on top of the clouds, which looked solid over all of England. I dropped out of formation and established a glide. I cut power to idle, put the main tanks on cross feed, and started the dead engine. The shortest course to England would bring us north and east of London.

I called Control for weather. They reported overcast with a ceiling of 500 feet. That presented a problem, as I needed an altitude of 700 feet for the crew to bail out successfully. The 500-foot ceiling meant the crew would have to leave the aircraft in "the soup."

When I was sure we were over England, I ordered the crew to bail out. They wanted to know what I was going to do. I told them I wanted to save the airplane. They refused to leave me and the aircraft, and I could not change their minds.

We were down to 500 feet when we dropped below the clouds. Woods and villages were all I could see in any direction. No airdrome was in sight. I couldn't believe it! There was no airfield.

At 400 feet I saw a B-26 followed by another, going down behind some trees. It had to be the American 9th Air Force Base. I pushed on the throttles to bring us around to line up for landing. I got one big burst of power, and then all engines stopped. God, it was quiet.

I headed for the base, not concerned about landing direction. I believed it would be preferable to land with gear down than to go in on the belly short of the field. We hit first in a potato field, went through a fence, and there was the airdrome. The runway ran north and south, and we were coming from the east. But we had a problem — we were going to cross the runway intersecting a B-26 landing.

I called the tower but got no response. At the last possible moment, the B-26 pilot saw us. He poured on the coal, jumped over us, and made another pattern. If he had not seen us, we would have collided.

We came off the runway on the west side. Directly ahead stood a concrete block with a jeep parked on it. Our left main gear hit the cement block at an angle, folding it back. The wing tip came down beside the jeep parked on the cement. We did a slow 90-degree turn and stopped.

A full Colonel walked up the wing and asked, "Do you have wounded on board?"

I said, "No, Sir."

He said, "Where were you today?"

I said, "Frankfurt. We're out of fuel." I told him, "I'm sorry for the trouble we're causing. Sure am glad the B-26 saw us and went around."

He said, "Think nothing of it. Come on down. I'll take care of your plane. You need a drink as does your crew. Take my jeep to the Club, and tell them to give you what you want. I'll be in when we get squared away."

He arrived at the Club a short time later. He had called our base and our Commander said to put us in a truck and ship us back that night. However, the Colonel said, "No, I'll send them on the next train in about an hour." He asked, "Do you realize you have full Tokyo tanks?"

I told him, "No."

On the way to the train, we stopped and checked our bird. Our transfer pump had taken a hit and was inoperable. We had 450 gallons of fuel that we could not use. I thought, with envy, about the capability of B-17s to gravity-feed the Tokyos into the mains.

I learned later that this Colonel received a promotion to Brigadier General. Then just before leaving for a Headquarters desk job, he went flying and crashed. He had been very decent to us. Too many good leaders were killed.

We had not been back on base a day when we were summoned to appear before the 8th Air Force Accident Board. The Board President, a Lieutenant Colonel, was not a pilot. My engineer and I were the only ones called to testify.

The Lieutenant Colonel was not aware that the B-24 had no gas gauges. When we finished testifying, he said, "Your actions as a Crew Commander were inadequate. What would you do to prevent a repeat of this accident?"

I was at a complete loss for something to say. Finally, I said, "Sir, I would pray."

He said, "I'm grounding you and your engineer." We saluted and left.

We joined the rest of our crew and went to our Squadron Commander's office. On the way, I checked the schedule. We were to fly a mission the next morning. The Commander told me to forget about the Accident Board; I did.

The 8th Air Force was changing tactics. It had a new Commander, Lieutenant General James Doolittle. The wind was now blowing a different direction. The 8th was on the offensive. The number of planes in the daily raids began to increase. Before General Doolittle had taken over, we had only put up 36 tops. After, each Group was putting up 55 birds for maximum effort.

At this time there was a series of lights over the Officers Club bar. The white light meant no mission the next day. We seldom saw that light. Next to it was a yellow light, which meant our Group had received an alert for a mission the following day. A blue light meant the mission plan and target was on station. Lead crews were to report to Intelligence and study the mission. When crews went to briefing, the green light went on. The last light was a red. It went on at takeoff and stayed on until the planes returned.

The bar closed at 2300 if any light other than white was on. We could tell from the lights what was going on; we knew when to drink and when not to.

We briefed for Frankfurt again on 4 February. It was to be a repeat of the earlier raid. The fires from the 9 January raid must have died down. The continent was clear, and we could drop visually. We had little damage from flak or fighters all the way to the IP some 35 miles northeast of our target.

On the run to the target, we took a flak burst in the bomb-bay area. I had not opened the bomb-bay doors; the flak burst punched holes in the incendiary bombs we were carrying.

A small fire was burning around the hydraulic lines and accumulator in the bomb bay itself, so I decided to pull the red handle and dump the burning bomb load. The bombs dropped through the doors, taking them off but getting rid of the biggest danger.

Two of the engines also took hits. The oil and cylinder head temperatures climbed rapidly and oil pressure dropped. I shut down the two engines and feathered the props while I still could. I knew I couldn't afford to become a straggler, as I would be easy meat for the German fighters to chew up.

I used my special screwdriver to crank up 65 inches of manifold pressure on the two good engines. We stayed in formation and did not attract the German fighters' attention. Several times the fire in the bomb bay sent a puff of smoke into the cockpit. It was lucky the bomb-bay doors were gone because with the doors attached and closed, one of those puffs would have been a fireball and we would have been a war statistic.

Over the Channel, we dropped out of formation. We needed to prepare for the landing. We would not have any hydraulic pressure to lower gear, drop flaps, or use brakes. We would have to hand crank the gear down. We managed to do that while we were still over the Channel, but it took longer than expected. We could see our field by the time we finished. I was positive all three wheels were down and locked.

I called the tower for permission to make a straight-in approach, but we couldn't crank down the flaps in time. I had put down the flap handle in case there was any pressure in the line to lower the flaps. But the pressure remained zero, and the flaps didn't go down. I had a habit of trying the brakes while on final, to be sure my feet were in proper position on the pedals.

When I reached the point where I felt we could make the runway, I called to Walt, "Cut the engines!" I forgot that I had braked after takeoff to stop wheel spin during retraction. I had thus trapped hydraulic pressure in the brake lines, and when I hit the brakes, the trapped pressure shot out into the flap line and dropped full flaps. I ballooned with four dead engines.

I let the plane stall and come down hard. We bounced, and went off the end of the runway, then bottomed to the belly in the muddy runway overrun. The mud filled the bomb-bay area, putting out the fire.

Other than digging out, all was well. The base Engineering Officer was first to arrive. He was angry about having to extricate the plane from the mud, but I told him that I didn't have time to rebuild the plane on final!

With only 5 missions completed against a fierce enemy, at that moment it didn't look promising to do 20 more, which was what it would take to complete a tour. Our American bombers contained guns that were superior defensively to any of Britain's bombers, and the United States also had a lot of fighters — more than the British. As a result, we did all of the day-time bombing, and the Royal Air Force handled the night raids. Together we did not give the major German targets any relief from attack, day or night.

Chapter 9

We got pretty good at bombing, and the Germans got pretty good at trying to stop us. But there was no way they could; there were too many of us. Our crews were getting cocky, and with good reason. We were no longer rookies. We were veterans who had been "down the pike."

The German fighters looked for stragglers, since they received as much credit for shooting down a cripple as they did for shooting down a healthy plane. And the cripples were a lot easier to kill. I made up my mind not to become a straggler.

On 11 February, we were awakened at 0200. We were to report for briefing after breakfast. On the way over to the Mess hall, I could not see my hand in front of my face. It was cold, damp, and foggy. No one thought a mission was possible. We had never taken off in such conditions. We figured we would brief, wait at the airplane, and see the red abort flares.

We endured the briefing. I didn't pay all that much attention to the target, a manufacturing and launching site for V-2 rockets. We were sure it was just another exercise in futility, as there had been so many other briefings when weather conditions were much better, and we had not flown.

At taxi time, a jeep with a light mounted on the back arrived; the light was up high so we could see it. The instructions were to follow the light, and it would lead us to takeoff position.

The mission by then had my full attention. We followed, and the light was all we could see in the fog. When we were on the runway, the jeep left.

We were to use the radio to take off. I told Walt Bulova, my copilot, to watch on the right side for the runway lights. He could see them as we passed. I went on instruments all the way, but I wanted to know if I was drifting to the right or left.

We cleared the ground, pulled up the gear and flaps, and established a climb. We went through a black cloud, and I knew someone had not made it.

I called the tower and requested a check on the planes already airborne. We were in the clear at 3,500 feet and climbing. Apparently it was an airplane from another base that had crashed.

We broke out into bright, beautiful sunshine as we climbed to join the other aircraft from our base. But only about one-third of the planes had gotten off. We formed a small Squadron and took up a heading for the target. We had little opposition going, good results at the target, and lost no one.

Clouds were solid up to 20,000 feet when we returned to England, and Control told us we could not land at our base nor possibly any other base in England. The only hope to land was to fly across England, out over the ocean to the west, then let down over the water, and fly back in on the deck to an RAF base on the west coast near the town of Ilfracombe. We had enough gas if we could find the field and make a quick landing.

Our lead Crew Commander decided we would let down and home in at one-minute intervals. When our lead determined that we were over the Atlantic, we dropped out of formation. We descended to just above the waves and flew on in toward land.

At 50 feet altitude, we could not see the water. I worried about going lower, however, relying only on an altimeter reading. There could be an error of 75 feet in a good altimeter properly set.

I dropped 10 feet at a time, and all crew members were staring into the fog to catch sight of the waves. At 20 feet above sea level, we barely were able to make out waves just below us. I had everyone looking while I went back on the gauges and homed on in.

Fortunately, the base had radar and called, "You're in line. Land from a straight-in approach. Call on sighting the runway." We never did see it, so I was very happy when the gear touched down.

We remained there overnight and flew home the next day through a snowstorm. Our field had about a foot of snow on the ground. We just wanted to get to the Club and have a few stiff drinks.

On 21 February 1944, we took off on mission number seven. We were to bomb an airfield in the heart of Germany. Our target was a factory producing aircraft whose airfield served as a working base for the Luftwaffe.

We suffered damage on the mission, dropped out of formation, and were going home down low to avoid being a straggler. A P-47 came alongside and the pilot asked, "Are you headed directly back to England?"

I said, "Yes, the sooner the better."

He replied, "Can I fly back with you? I have damage." He was trailing smoke. I suspected he did not know where he was.

I told him to tuck in under us and we would lead him to one of our emergency strips. We would get fuel there, and he could get help. He thanked us and then sat right down under our wing.

We told him to land first, which he was happy to do. Afterwards, we met him in Operations. He was only 17 years old; his voice had barely changed. This man could not get a driver's license in some states, but he could go to war, fly a Jug, and fight for his country.

I had to laugh at our Intelligence people. They would describe the flak in the target area one day as "a meager concentration of light flak." The next day they would say "a light concentration of meager flak." At the "charm school" for Intelligence officers, they learned to vary their speech that way. Most would not have known a flak gun if they had tripped over one. We paid little attention to them.

After each mission, we wrote up the airplane and listed everything that required repair. Then we went in and sat at a table with one of the Intelligence officers. If we tried to tell them something new, they questioned our sanity.

They often used their authority to recommend crews for what we called the

Chapter 9

"flak house." Flak houses were large homes where you could spend a week or two in peace and quiet. Those sent enjoyed the rest, and the food was good. However, it delayed finishing a tour, and I wanted no part of such a place.

We almost got sent to a flak house when we tried to tell Intelligence that the German fighters were firing cannon shells with proximity fuses. On clear days when we were on missions, we had seen rockets come up from the ground. They spiraled upward and passed through the formation. They seldom hit anything. We called them scarecrows. However, the Intelligence community was positive that such shells did not exist. So making a report on the ground-to-air rockets could earn the crew a trip to the "flak house." In reality, the Germans used the rockets for months before anyone in authority acknowledged that they existed.

The culmination of all this was when the Germans began flying the ME-262 jets and the ME-263 rocket fighters. We reported sighting those planes, but it took most of a year to convince Intelligence that they actually existed. They were much faster than anything else in the sky.

We soon learned that reporting new items was a ticket to a head shrinker. They thought everyone was nuts. We were. If not, we wouldn't have been in that war.

We learned to report, "As briefed." After debriefing, each crew member received a jigger of bourbon. If he made no waves, he got to his whiskey much more quickly. Sometimes you could get another jigger from someone who did not drink.

On the Hesepe raid, a friend from our Squadron got hit badly on the bomb run, losing two engines. But he managed to hold position and drop on target. After the bomb run, he went into a dive to avoid becoming a straggler. He hoped to make it home on the deck. The Germans had seen him, however, and were waiting. Five FW-190s followed and poured it to him with cannons and .50-caliber guns. Two gunners died instantly, and two other crewmen bailed out. They reached the deck, and the Germans still fired into them again and again.

The plane was over Holland by that time and flying just off the ground on two engines. A cannon burst took out the instrument panel and all the instruments except the needle and ball. The only operable item was the magnetic compass. But the remaining crew made it to the coast, and the Germans ran out of ammunition. One of the Germans pulled up alongside the aircraft and saluted them as if to say, "Good luck. We missed you this time, but we'll get you next time."

By the grace of God, they got across the Channel. They made it to our field, and went off the runway and into the mud upon landing. But they were home at last. Only one engine was up to speed at the end. The pilot, Hervey Broxten, and his crew did a distinguished job of getting back.

Chapter 10

On 24 February 1944, we were awakened at 0130. Breakfast at 0200 was ridiculous, especially a breakfast of powdered eggs and burned toast. We sat at a table with Moose Tarrant and his crew. Moose was a lot like me in trying to fly not only to do the job but more importantly to live. Moose ended the conversation with the comment, "Can you imagine those German radar operators today watching our two blips on their screens? They're bound to ask, 'Are those two crazy bastards still flying over here?'" A good chuckle before briefing is a tonic for the whole day. Moose always could raise our morale.

Somehow, that day the air felt electrically charged. Normally that signified a long, deep penetration into Fortress Europe. But it was a bit of a different feeling on the 24th as we filed into the briefing. One of the chaplains began with a prayer. Then came the unveiling of the big map showing our target and route. It was a deep penetration to an airfield and factory complex at Gotha, Germany. Our Group was well back in the bomber stream.

During check-out our plane performed like a good one, all ready and willing to do its job. It was a late model, silver, with no signs of battle damage. We were airborne a bit after 0600. We climbed to altitude on the race-track course. We had only one near miss while climbing — a good start for the day.

We spent more than two hours flying around England while the bomber stream formed. On a clear day our contrails would by then have made the day overcast. The contrails from well over 1,000 Heavy bombers from the 8th Air Force, along with another 500 Medium bombers from the 9th, filled the sky. Then increase these with another 500 flights from each force escorting and making fighter sweeps. Coming out of Italy most days were nearly 1,000 bombers and their escort of fighters. Add to this the smoke from bombs on many targets and burning aircraft from the Luftwaffe, and a clear day becomes overcast.

As we crossed the coast, the German gunners sent up some flak. They were not expecting to hit us, but wanted to wake us up to the fact that we were now entering their territory. An hour later when we crossed into Germany itself, we could see much action ahead.

The Germans had their Luftwaffe in the air going after the bombers. Everywhere we looked, there were planes spiraling down, trailing smoke and flames. Some planes and crews were ours, but many were German.

Some crews were able to bail out, but many went down with their planes as they blew up in massive explosions, filling the sky with debris. As we approached the target, the Germans were landing to refuel; we made the bomb run without getting hit by fighters. We were carrying 16 500-pound general-purpose bombs, a normal load for hitting an airfield, factory, and hangars.

We had a K-24 camera mounted in the waist, facing down. We could use it to follow the bombs from our plane to the target. Art loved to watch the results. I never saw anyone get more excited than he did. One time he tracked a bomb and watched it hit a fighter landing on a runway; the explosion ended the war for that pilot. But we did not get off easy; the Germans came up and hit us on our way out.

We hoped the film would print and show the result. It did. Art got credit for a kill and lorded it over the rest of us. He hoped all of our targets would be airfields so he could become the first "bombardier ace" of the war. We led our Group the next day; we were carrying demolition bombs. The Initial Point for the bomb run began from a specific shaped woods, river, and town. The IP was some 50 miles northwest of Furth. We flew into heavy flak. A good friend of mine, Charlie Billings, took a bad hit, and he had no choice but to pull the red handle and salvo his bomb load.

It was a clear day, and we watched Charlie's bombs fall and hit in the woods filled with ammunition, bombs, and other explosives. The resulting blast defied description. We were flying at 28,000 feet, and the force raised us up a good 200 more. Giant fires erupted from the woods; black smoke billowed and plumed out at 50,000 feet.

Crews with hand-held cameras took pictures. Everyone returning chuckled at the debriefing. Ironically, the damage accidentally created from the ammo storage in the woods probably exceeded that done to the target.

Headquarters rewrote our orders to include the ammunition dump in the target area, permitting official credit for its destruction, though no one had known it existed. But the Germans would think we knew. It was an Intelligence game. Charlie eventually made it back safely and gained quite a reputation.

The first big raid on Berlin came on 5 March. I went on the raid, and the weather was horrible. There was a lot of dangerous flying, but no brass ring. A single Group of B-17s climbed to 33,000 to stay on top of the clouds, and they made it to Berlin. The B-24s could not climb above 28,000 feet, so they hit Hamburg as a secondary target. We never got on top, and Headquarters called us back.

Again the next morning we left for Berlin. We got our first taste of the barrage flak protecting the German capital. It was so thick we could walk on it. It was a wonder anyone made it through, but most did. We accepted our losses. Those who made it back to England were grateful.

By this time our Group needed replacement crews. We found ourselves flying back-to-back missions; replacements were not coming in fast enough.

On 8 March, we returned to Berlin. The Erkner Werks on the outskirts of town was our target. I took stock of our situation, and it was grim. I knew I had to fly better if we were to survive, and our gunners had to shoot sooner. They had to have their guns trained on the fighters as soon as they were visible. I had to fly tighter formation when fighters were around, but I had to loosen the formation and take evasive action against all flak, even on the bomb run.

I was not alone. Many others were aware of the need for these same tactics. We began to think for ourselves and fly by principles so that we could survive. We improved. Our Group began to look good.

Many new Groups were flying and were getting hit as we had months earlier. On occasion, the Germans left *us* alone to chase newer and easier meat.

The Charge of Quarters woke me the next morning, the 9th, and said, "Skip breakfast and report to Operations now." A pilot had suffered an attack of appendicitis and had been rushed to the hospital for surgery. Our Squadron Commander had selected me to fly his crew.

I didn't want to fly another crew and doubted that they wanted a stranger for their aircraft Commander either. I knew it would displease my crew, as they would have to fly one with someone else. I was afraid of this flight, and although I could have refused, I didn't.

This was my twelfth mission, and the target was Neinberg. On the way in, German fighters hit us. We flew on the low left and two German fighters set up their scissors attack on our tail. They climbed about 1,500 feet above us, spread wide right and left. Then they attacked, crossing at about their cannon-firing range, climbed back up, and hit us again.

A cannon shell hit our tail turret and made it inoperable. The gunner could point the guns but he was unable to fire. He wanted to leave the turret, but I

Chapter 10

told him to stay and call me when the Germans started their run.

I called our lead, telling him I was climbing over the top. The other planes in our Group could shoot at the Germans as they attacked us. We repeated the procedure a good 20 times. The fighters finally left, most likely because they were low on fuel.

The crew probably thought I was nuts. They acted as if they were happy to get home in one piece. We had a three-day pass to London, then, so I took in some shows, hit a few bars, and ate a lot. I also did a great deal of thinking. I came to the conclusion that I should take more evasive action and stop making it easy for the Germans.

On 20 March, we hit Frankfurt again, the hub of central Germany. Major autobahns ran east to west and north to south through the city. It was the location of the largest cartels in the world, a major communications center for telephone and telegraph, and for rail and air movements. We were told to do a good enough job so that we would not have to return. We had done a good job on the previous trips. Each time we hit an entirely different target within the Frankfurt complex.

As usual, the Germans threw up the flak. I managed to turn back into the bursts. It worked like a charm. I was doing evasive action in formation, and it was proving to be effective. We had good bomb results. Flying in combat began to click for our crew and others, but our bombing results were better than those of the other Groups. Up to this point, we had been only average or below.

Operations sent a new Crew Commander to fly as copilot with us. The loss of new crews on first missions had reached alarming levels. Headquarters thought this procedure might help reduce those losses. I tried to explain to him what we did and why, though I sensed he was not paying attention. He spent most of the time telling me how his crew was going to set a record shooting down German fighters. He had an obsession about that.

I tried to tell him that a B-24 was no match for a good fighter with cannon and fixed guns. But he remained convinced that he and his crew could whip the Luftwaffe all by themselves. I had serious doubts about their longevity in combat.

Two days later we were once again on the way to Berlin. The pilot who had gone with us to Frankfurt was flying his first mission with his own crew. We were to cross an IP north of Berlin and make the bomb run heading south. The field order assigned our Group well back in the bomber stream.

Some congestion occurred at the IP. We flew farther to the northeast to provide spacing. The new crew was flying on the outside low left. I saw them deliberately begin to drop back on the turn. We watched a group of ME-109s holding northeast, deciding which bombers to hit and when. Our wide turn provided targets, and down they came.

I called the new crew and tried to get them to close up. They ignored my advice. The pilot said, "You watch us. We'll show you how to shoot down German fighters."

Less than a minute later, they were trailing smoke from a couple of engines and dropping to the northeast. I felt sick. That didn't have to have happened. We went on to the target and had a good bomb pattern. The flak was heavy, but our losses were light.

The fighters hit again as we cleared the target area, but we were in tight formation and stood them off.

The Germans by then had both V-1 and V-2 rockets and were constructing launch facilities for them. The next raid, our fifteenth, was to Mozenville, France, to hit one of these. The mission was a big morale booster because the Germans had not put up any good defense.

On 29 March, we flew a "no ball," as we code-named it, to Watten, France, hitting a completed V-1 launch facility. We flew over the target at 14,000 feet on the first no ball. By this time the Germans had good defenses, and we suffered a lot of damage. Our altitude was ideal for the German 88mm flak, and they had a good day. It was the last raid we made on no ball targets at those ridiculous altitudes.

On the way back, we spotted a large U.S. Navy convoy sailing in the Channel to the south of our course. My Squadron Commander was leading. He called and said, "Why not show them we're here doing our stuff?"

Everyone thought it was a good idea, so we turned south and started a letdown. As soon as we were in range, the ships opened fire on us. We were down to 3,000 feet, so it was no joke. Everyone called and tried to tell them who we were. But the Navy paid no attention; they shot at anything, friend or foe. We ended up going every man for himself, taking maximum evasive action. Our own Navy was trying to shoot us down!

Captain Black and his crew shared our hut at Seething. He kept our agreement not to fly the same missions so that if one of us turned up missing, the other would fly over the Channel and search for the downed plane. Since he was the Assistant Operations Officer, he could arrange our schedules that way. On 1 April 1944 he and his crew flew a raid into the heart of Germany.

We went down to Operations to watch the planes return. Black's crew was missing. I asked returning crews if they had seen him get hit. At least ten crews said that he was crossing the Rhine River when his plane got hit by flak. Nine or ten chutes had come out as the plane spiraled down. I went to our Squadron Commander who assigned me a plane to fly out and look for them. Then I decided it would be foolish to fly out over the Channel because apparently he had not reached it.

A week later we heard that Captain Black's crew *had* gone down in the Channel. A fishing boat had found them on 6 April. Air/sea rescue had picked them up, and they were in a hospital near our base. I felt sick because I had not gone out to look for them. Our Squadron Commander let us use a car to go to the hospital where we found them all in one room. They had gotten hit crossing the Rhine River and tried to make it home. Only one engine was putting out anything resembling full power, and they ditched about a mile offshore.

Eight of the ten-man crew had survived. The copilot could not swim. They could not get him to the raft alive. Another man had died the second day from exposure and injuries. They said morale had been good until after dark on the first day because they believed I would find them. I had never felt lower. I told them what had happened. They said they understood and showed no resentment.

They left the hospital two weeks later, scheduled to come by the base, pick up their gear, and return to the States. On 20 April, they returned for a day and night. Everyone gathered in our hut for a party. All liquid refreshments had disappeared by 0200, but the party continued, and many called for drinks.

Captain Black and I went to the Club to get someone to sell us more refreshments, but we couldn't wake up anyone. So we pushed in the door to the storage room and rolled a barrel of beer to our hut. The party went on until the sun was coming up. Then everyone drifted off to his hut to get some sleep.

The next afternoon, a call came over the loudspeaker for all officers to assemble in the Club. As we entered, we saw the door to the storage room sitting on the stage as Exhibit A. The new Group Commander, Colonel Mason, began with a talk about conduct overseas. It seemed he had tried all day to find out who the culprits were.

I thought at first I would stand up and end the suspense. However, second thoughts made me decide to go over to his quarters later and tell him. After I explained what had happened and admitted to taking the beer, he said, "I appreciate your coming over. It's out of my hands. The staff has already filed charges. You will list all who were in on the party."

I said, "I can't do that. It will be up to each of them to decide what he wants to do. I can only speak for myself."

The Commander told me I was under arrest in my quarters. I could go to eat in the Mess, but otherwise could only leave quarters to fly missions. Court-martial charges had been sent to the 8th Air Force.

I returned to my hut to begin my imprisonment. Crews walking past threw rocks at the hut and shouted, "How goes it in jail?" No one else ever confessed.

On 22 April we briefed to bomb Hamm, Germany. Afterward we were held there until trucks arrived at noon to take us to the Mess. About four in the afternoon we received an "all clear" to fly. We flew over the target at dusk. All went well, and we left the target as night set in. We discussed whether to fly home individually or in formation, then decided on the latter with our running and formation lights on.

As we reached the coast area, another B-24 Group was flying to our left. A plane in that Group was in trouble. An engine was on fire, and the flames were getting larger and spreading.

A P-47 was flying down below the crippled B-24 and was telling the pilot how it looked. The Jug pilot doubted that the B-24 could make it. He recommended the crew bail out. The bomber pilot agreed, but only nine left the aircraft. He told the Jug pilot that one chute had been hit and ruined, and thus one man couldn't go. He was going to try to make it home.

The P-47 pilot said, "Please try to crash-land on the coast. I'll cover you."

The B-24 pilot gave his name, his wife's name, and his home address, then asked the Jug pilot to write his wife. "Tell her I only did what I had to do." He wasn't sorry.

The Jug pilot moved out as flames spread into the wing. The bomber pilot said, "Please contact my Group and tell them I loved flying with them. They're tops in my book."

There was a giant fireball, and a brave man died.

As we crossed the Channel we broke out at the buncher into six-ship elements to descend, then singly to land. I was leading the bucket, flying just below the lead element as we crossed the coast. Suddenly the left wing off the lead burst into flames. He nosed over almost straight down and went into the Channel. I thought at first that someone had lit a cigarette and ignited gas fumes. Then my right wing blew up from tracers and bullets hitting him.

I knew that we had stopped using tracers, and realized at that point that some of the planes had only two exhaust stacks. They had to be German twin-engine fighters, and they must have come back with us.

We broke off to make a straight-in approach to base. Captain Skaggs was leading. Someone began shooting at him from what appeared to be the top turrets of planes on our base as he came down on final. Actually they were shooting at us from their own gun emplacements around the base.

I thought of the cannons we had brought from Florida. They had been mounted on top of Group Headquarters. What irony it would be if we got shot down over our own airfield, especially if the guns were the ones we had brought over ourselves. I made a quick decision. I climbed back to altitude and turned off all lights.

From then on, bombers were shooting at bombers. The British scrambled their night fighters. Searchlights came on, and flak batteries began shooting at anything. Planes were burning all over the area. It was complete confusion. We got into the searchlights once, and flak began to come up. I did all I could to finally break out of the lights.

We flew around England for two hours while things calmed down. I called

Chapter 10

for a fix and steer as we were not sure where we were.

A voice speaking in English told me to fly 90 degrees for 30 minutes. I knew that would put us beyond our base because I could see the Channel. I realized that the person talking was a German who was trying to sucker us right into Germany.

I called our tower and asked them to turn on the landing lights. I said, "I am Addle D Dog."

They said, "Addle D Dog got shot down."

I gave my serial number, the score of the World Series games, and details of the Army-Navy football game. They would not comply.

Someone in another tower called and said, "We believe you. We're turning on our lights." On came the lights at three bases. I picked the middle base and landed. Going down the runway, I saw planes from several different Groups off to the side. We didn't know what field we were on.

When we were parked, we found that we were on our own field, and we were very happy to be there. We learned that Captain Skaggs had taken a bad hit on final approach. A main line in the bomb-bay area was severed, cutting fuel to all engines. His engineer went into the bomb bay and held the hose ends together which allowed the engines to run long enough to get to the runway. They ran off the side and went down in the mud. The engineer became trapped in the bomb bay of the burning B-24. He dug his way out, tearing most of the flesh from his hands.

We learned later that only three to five German planes had come in. One went down near our base. A Squadron Commander wearing a Class-A uniform was flying that plane.

About 80 B-24s had blown up, burned, or crashed. Most of the damage was the result of our shooting at each other or shots fired from our own bases although some planes were shot down by the British. The Germans shot down at most three or four. Command only reported the losses the enemy could confirm. The record listed a loss of four planes.

Chapter 11

Combat had a way of making people superstitious. We laughed about it, but we actually believed and followed the myths we had created.

Many wrote "last letters" and left them with a friend to mail if they did not return from a raid. All too often they did fail to return. Friends had to send far too many letters. I didn't write to my wife once I appeared on the schedule to fly. I believed that God would let me live to write to Jeri after the raid. It must have worked, because I survived. It was one of my superstitions.

Another was sitting on my hat during a mission. It became a ritual for the entire crew. Before we took off, they always asked if I was sitting on my hat. It developed a first-class 50-mission crush.

Sitting around in a steel hut got old in a hurry. By 24 April, I had had enough of the arrest in quarters. I assembled my crew and told them how I felt. I wanted us on the schedule to fly daily. If we were not going to survive anyway, why waste time on a court-martial? We couldn't go anywhere but to Mess and on missions, so we might as well fly. The crew agreed.

I went to see the Group Commander and presented my case. Colonel Mason called our Squadron Commander. He said, "Fly Swayze's crew on every mission. He's here now and will report to you at once."

Our target the following day was Mannheim, Germany. The German flak in the target area was heavy and accurate. Their fighters hit us on the way to the target and on the way home as well.

Chapter 11

I was flying better, and we had no problems. We had many crews with more than ten missions and were not losing the older ones, though overall losses reached more than six percent each mission.

We were up early on 27 April for another no-ball target. The Germans had established good defenses around these targets, and the missions were no longer considered "milk runs." We landed back at Seething by noon. Ten of our crews from the first mission joined a contingent of crews and flew a second strike in the afternoon to a new target. It was the first "two-in-one-day" operation, which soon became known as "two for one." But we got credit for only one — our nineteenth mission. The worst blow, however, came when we returned and learned that Headquarters had announced that our tours had increased to 30 missions.

Being under arrest and confined to quarters had cut my morale. Then to fly two missions and get credit for only one had also irritated me. Having my tour extended rubbed salt into the wound. I was as near to true bitterness as I had ever been.

To me, set tours were wrong, a complete dereliction of duty on the part of the Commanders. Some crews could go on and on; others ran out of gas early. Some crews had devastating missions; others lucked out and flew easy missions with only minor problems. Crews having members maimed or killed bore a heavier load than the luckier ones who suffered no casualties. The rationale for a set number of missions was beyond me.

We flew another deep penetration to Berlin on 29 April. We were attacked by the "Abbeyville Kids" — a crack Luftwaffe fighter unit — in their yellow-nosed birds. Our plane remained untouched in the fray, our twentieth mission. The mission on 30 April got scrubbed because of poor weather over the continent. Then on 1 May, we flew to bomb Brussels, Belgium. We were over the continent heading for the target when we received the recall; we had no choice but to return home. We couldn't see the assigned target for a visual bomb run, and rules prevented the random bombing of targets of opportunity in friendly nations.

We landed, ate lunch, and went on an afternoon raid. The weather had moved east, and the Brussels target was now visible; we were to bomb the marshaling yards.

I seldom got a good view of the target after the bombs hit. But on this mission our course changed direction, allowing me to look down the bomb bay and watch the whole show. We had a near-perfect bomb pattern. The exploding bombs blew rail cars into the air. Many exploded, turning them and their contents into dust and small bits of debris. The cars had obviously contained munitions that the Germans would never use to kill our ground forces. The devastation was something to witness. I was happy to be on the sending end and not receiving.

B-24s of the 715th Squadron crossing the English Channel to bomb Germany.

Chapter 11

The weather was bad throughout the spring in 1944. Summer refused to arrive. Weather grounded the 8th Air Force until 6 May when we flew to Sira Court, France. The flak was as heavy and as accurate as at any German target. We were happy when we got out of its range. The fire was heavy, accurate, and close enough to see the big orange and red centers of the bursts. The shrapnel sounded like someone peppering the bottom of the airplane with gravel.

We hit Muenster in the Ruhr on 7 May and once again met heavy flak over the target. Our plane went untouched, and we returned home with all four engines turning. Then came three days of bad weather giving us a rest. During this period we received word that Headquarters had reversed its thinking and would allow mission credit for second raids flown on a single day. This decision improved morale among the crews; it also helped restore faith in our Headquarters personnel.

On 11 May we hit the communications center in Mulhouse. We had noticed that our targets had begun to change. We were now hitting communications and transportation facilities, not just factories and aircraft facilities.

On our way in and out daily, we had watched the build-up of Army organizations in southern England. There could be little doubt that an invasion would come soon. Otherwise, England was going to sink from the weight of the equipment and forces stationed there!

We bombed the marshaling yard in Bohlen on 12 May. A train in the yard, loaded with mines, would have left soon for the coastal area around Normandy. That was our twenty-fifth mission. We felt it should have been the end of our tour.

On 22 May we returned to the Sira Court launch area with two 1,000-pound bombs set to pierce armor. The target survived the 500- and 1,000-pound bombs dropped on the launchers; the Germans repaired them and began firing into London again.

We hit a big German airfield southwest of Paris on 23 May. We felt this had to be more preparation for the invasion. It was not a rough mission, but I did see three of our planes go down.

We did two for one again on 25 May, bombing the Mulhouse marshaling yard in the morning and flying a no-ball mission in the afternoon to Fecamp, France. On 26 May we got a welcomed rest because of bad weather. On 27 May we flew a long haul to Koblenz, Germany. Then we had another day off because of bad weather.

On 29 May we flew a long haul to Tutow, Germany, and destroyed an aircraft factory. This mission made us wonder just how close we were to an invasion. The intent of the planners confused us; it had to puzzle the Germans as well.

Our forming procedures were standard. We took off, homed on a beacon, and climbed on a race-track course. On top, the lead and special forming ships

First Lieut. Jack Swayze of Seattle (right), pilot of a Liberator bomber with the Eighth Air Force, and two members of his ship's crew are shown here at an advanced French base loading into their Liberator the canopy of a Messerschmitt-109, which they are taking home as a souvenir. At the left is 1st Lieut. Joe Apicella, Roosevelt, N. Y., and inside the plane is Arthur O. Archambault, Onesachet, R. I.

Jack Swayze (left) assisting in the delivery of food for Paris, France, 1944. (The newspaper caption has the individual identifications switched.)

circled and fired flares. Each Group had special colors for identification. It was frightening to climb. We would barely miss other climbing planes with no chance to dodge. I hated it. The near misses, while climbing in weather, took more off of our lives than combat.

I met and talked to a B-17 tail gunner in London who was in the turret while they climbed. He could not wear a chute in the turret, so he kept it just outside the area, on the deck. On one mission he felt something was wrong as they climbed; he decided to check on his chute. When he opened the turret door, the airplane was not there. The tail had separated from the main body. They had collided with another airplane, cutting theirs in half. His chute and the rest of his plane had disappeared. All he could do was close the door and ride it down. The tail section floated down and crashed in a field. He escaped without serious injury, but Headquarters concluded he had had enough; they sent him home. The good Lord was on his side. I could believe nothing short of his having experienced a miracle.

After hearing this story, I decided I had climbed the race-track course long enough and that I would fly directly out over the Channel, fly to Control Point "A," and circle until our Group arrived. Then I would join up, having avoided the near misses in the climbout and the forming area. We had flown 29 missions and worried that Headquarters might increase the mission requirement again.

The weather was miserable on 30 May, so the mission was canceled. On 31 May, we took off in bad weather to hit a launch site at Woippy, France. We couldn't make a visual run and had to abort the mission. Consequently, we didn't receive mission credit. We had flown through a lot of flak for nothing — all in a day's work.

The Acting Assistant Operations Officer told me he wanted to start flying again to complete his tour, so on 2 June I asked him to fly with me. For some reason I felt that I wanted to have him along to fly the bird home after exiting the continent. I believed it would be wise to have a witness — a witness for what, I didn't know! It turned out to be a premonition.

Our target was Beauvoir, France. It was a fine mission with no problems from the enemy. When we crossed over the Channel on the way home, I climbed out of the seat and let Charlie take over. He flew us home and made a perfect landing. I was pleased; our tour was over. We were the first crew in our Squadron to complete one.

When we went to critique, I was told to report to the Group Commander. I went in and saluted. He said, "You radioed you would be at three feet in three minutes. You were over the field, and regulations require you to land normally and not buzz. You've committed a court-martial offense."

This was it! They were out to get me. Thank God I had asked Captain Billings to fly with me. I told the Commander that I had left the pilot's seat at the French coast, that Captain Billings had flown the plane on home and landed. I said, "We didn't buzz, nor did we call the tower."

The Commander got up and left the room. He returned in 10 or 15 minutes and offered congratulations on our being the first crew in our Squadron to finish a tour. I could tell his heart was not in what he was saying.

The crew that was shot down after boasting that they would set a record shooting down Germans returned to our base. They were wearing new German suits and were picking up their gear to go back to the States. They had descended after their plane was hit and then bailed out. They had slept the first night in haystacks, but by morning, the Germans were burning them. While poor people in an area usually would help, they often lacked the means. So the crew had decided to pick the richest-looking house. They told the occupants who they were and had asked for help in escaping.

Luckily, the people were wealthy Danes whose sympathies were with the Allies. They had sheltered the crew, provided new clothes, and arranged for their transport to Sweden. Had the men entered Sweden in uniform, the authorities would have interned them for the duration of the war. Because they wore civilian clothes, they were not held as military personnel and were allowed to leave the country. The Swedes had sent them back to England.

The crew could have returned to flying, but because they had been in German territory, they would be executed as spies if they went down again and were caught. The rules of combat sent them back to the States; the war was over for them.

Chapter 12

One night the British bombed Hamburg with maximum force. The following morning the 8th Air Force also bombed the city. The combined efforts produced a fire storm. Winds in the streets exceeded 200 miles an hour. The destruction was inconceivable. More than 80,000 people lost their lives in the raid and its resulting fire storm.

Bomber Command's missions preceding the D-Day invasion on 6 June 1944 were part of the Allied air offensive of Europe. Targets were airfields, aircraft plants, ball-bearing plants, oil refineries, and other strategic items. As the invasion neared, the targets became more transportation and communications related. Fuel storage facilities, refineries, marshaling yards, and other transportation facilities became a priority.

When more and more communications targets began to appear, we knew that the invasion was imminent. At the same time, Americans emphasized hitting military targets only, whereas the British didn't much care if civilian workers lost their lives when a factory was destroyed. Having suffered through the German bombings of London and Coventry, they apparently cared little about whom or what they hit with their bombs as long as it hastened the day of Germany's downfall.

On one of our early passes to London, we had stayed at the Red Cross hostel, the only place we could afford. It charged only enough to meet costs, not to make a profit. The rooms were clean, adequate, and appreciated. One of the last big German raids on London came that night. Several hundred German bombers suddenly were overhead. It was quite an experience when they dropped their bombs with sirens and whistles attached. The noise was dreadful. Bombs alone were bad enough — this was ludicrous.

The British had antiaircraft batteries all over London. Every park bristled with guns. But everything they shot into the air fell back to earth, so there was an immense amount of falling debris which could kill anyone or anything it hit.

We had to watch the show. There were hundreds of searchlights and antiaircraft guns firing. The sky clouded over with German bombers, night fighters, and bombs. It was something to see. The subway tunnels served as air raid shelters; they were full at all levels during the raid. It was a sobering experience to see entire families living there. They used canned heat to cook what little food they could get. There were children four and five years old who knew no other home. How they ever managed to sleep on concrete among the crowds was a mystery to me. It made me want to return to our base, fly missions, and bring this devastating war to an end.

Our Headquarters had gathered information on crews and losses. We were not losing many crews after they had flown their tenth mission, but the loss rate went up for crews flying their final five. It seemed that experience was an important factor in survival. But I still believed a tour of duty tied to a set number of missions was not a good idea. Some crews could handle flying indefinitely; others could not. It was an individual matter.

The human mind develops strange patterns to survive in combat. Each could cope with only so much fear, destruction, and gore. After that, the mind rejected what was going on in plain view. Then a sense of detached unreality took over, and the war was seen from some disjoined perspective.

While the Air Forces loss rate had settled in at slightly more than 6 percent per mission, the number of missions required to complete a tour rose to 35. That seemed to me to translate into a loss rate of 210 percent during a crew's tour!

The odds for any crew finishing a tour were slim to none. Only 5 of my Squadron's 18 original crews finished their tour, and our Group stood above the average in the 8th Air Force. Those of us with families knew that the ones paying the price for the war were the wives and families, especially those who lost fathers, sons, and husbands. The women had to adjust somehow and keep family life in order. Often all they received was a piece of paper telling them of the heroism of their missing or killed family member.

Rumors were running rampant about the planned invasion. Much was pure speculation, but we thought where there was smoke, there had to be some fire.

Headquarters offered me an opportunity to fly a mission with a Royal Air Force crew in a Lancaster bomber. I would receive mission credit. I seriously considered accepting. I felt responsible for my people, and I knew it was mutual. Yet, I could not shake the feeling that going out of one's way into danger was foolhardy. I believed that I should only put at risk the personnel needed to accomplish the mission. This one was not mission essential.

On 3 June I reported to the Group Commander's office. He handed me a letter from the Commanding General of the 8th Air Force. It contained the papers that had been filed to court-martial me for breaking down the door earlier and taking the keg of beer. A letter said, "We have an important mission to perform over here. We cannot court-martial those who get thirsty during the night." The signature was that of General Doolittle, Commander, 8th Air Force.

The Group Commander told me I would be fined up to half a month's pay in place of the court-martial. I didn't know military law, or I would have told him to shove it. In effect, he fined my wife $100.

Shortly after that, one evening a crew from a nearby hut came over to tell me that the mission tomorrow would be their twentieth. They had decided there was no way they could make it through the next ten, so they were going to the nearest neutral country. They wanted us to know. We talked far into the night, but they wouldn't change their minds.

I lay awake thinking and concluded that they were the only ones who knew if they had really reached the breaking point. If that's what they had decided, I would say nothing.

So many crews had gone to neutral countries that the Army Air Forces had published a directive against flying to them in formation! On a Berlin raid one day, I had watched three B-24 aircraft leave formation, each with four fans turning. They had joined three B-17s heading for Sweden, which also had all four fans turning. So I knew engine trouble wasn't their problem.

I watched the crew that I had talked to the night before. They were in position on the bomb run. Then we all got busy and I did not see what happened to them. They didn't return, but did show up later on the list of those interned in Switzerland. I didn't know whether they had received damage, making it necessary to go into a neutral base. But their failure to return triggered an investigation because so many others had gone to neutral countries. The investigating officer knew the crew had taken Class-A uniforms and B-4 bags. I told him they always took those on missions. I said, "They didn't have any reason to look at the mission any differently from previous missions. Why would anyone with twenty missions want to quit?" He may have thought I had a point. The word came down later that the Air Forces figured that if a crew had flown seven raids, it had paid for the cost of training.

Later in the morning, we took off to hit Berlin. It was a rough mission. Fighters hit us before the IP, and a massive flak barrage came up as we reached the target. We lost several planes to fighters and flak, and all others received damage.

We often listened to either Radio Berlin or Radio Bremen. Berlin had a disk jockey called "Berlin Betty," while "Midge" broadcast from Bremen. They both played the latest hits of American bands. If anyone wanted to hear Harry James, the Dorsey Brothers, or Glenn Miller, he listened to the German propaganda stations. But between songs, the German disk jockeys told us our girlfriends and wives were out having a ball with the Jews and that all we crewmen had to look forward to was a cot in Stalag 13. We also loved to listen to German propagandist Lord Haw Haw who raised our morale.

We had not been in England a week before the German stations had broadcast our unit designation and location. They had told where we had been in the States. They knew the names of the Commanders and their hometowns. They gave the names of those captured each day. But none of that bothered us; we listened anyway. The broadcasts lifted our morale instead of destroying it. Propaganda seldom worked as the sender hoped or believed.

For each man flying, it took about ten support personnel primarily in maintenance, supply, and armament. Those men worked their rears off to keep us in the air. When we landed late in the afternoon, many aircraft required repair. Support personnel had to load and check all guns. Each plane had to receive a new load of bombs which had to be double-checked and fuzed. The men loaded and insured the fuel load for each plane; often they worked all night in the most disagreeable weather. We never heard a single complaint from any of them.

Winters in England were wet, snowy, and always cold — a damp cold that penetrated to the bone. After working all night, the support personnel came down late in the afternoon to watch the crews and planes return. They stared off to the east to catch the first sight of our planes. They counted them and knew how many were missing. They took pride in their work and wanted to see their plane come back. They wanted all the crews to be safe. On days when losses were high, their faces reflected their sorrow. Those men received little credit and much criticism, and lived a tough life. There was no set tour for them. They were there for the duration, no matter how long it might take. Their pay was only a pittance considering the work they did, because without them, victory could not happen; the invasion would fail.

Everyone watching the returning planes knew the meaning of the flares that were fired. Red flares meant wounded on board and a call for an ambulance. Yellow flares meant the plane had serious damage and mechanical problems and was calling for priority in landing. Those who fired no flares gave landing priority to planes with wounded aboard or mechanical problems. There were many days when nearly all of the planes fired flares.

A good friend of mine was flying the forming ship one morning. When they returned, he did a buzz job to make sure everyone was awake for the day. He

Chapter 12

got a little low on one pass and took out a limb on one of the Queen's trees. It passed through the wall of our Group Commander's office and bounced off his desk. After my friend's tour, he was assigned to Ireland for the duration on the field where all replacement crews reported. To me that seemed unjust. That Commander was not one of my favorite persons.

We rode the bus to meet the Reassignment Board at Division Headquarters on 4 June 1944. Ours was the first crew in our Squadron to finish a tour. We didn't know what to expect.

I met with the Board first and was given several options. I could stay for another 90 days, go to another Group, or be an instructor, which could result in a promotion — but there were no guarantees. Or, I could be sent home for 30 days' rest and recuperation, then return and fly a second tour. This option would send me home for reassignment. I had five minutes to decide, so I did some fast thinking. I knew I wanted to stay in the Air Forces. A second tour sounded good toward making a career, and I thought going home to stay was leaving a job unfinished. I also didn't want to leave all my friends still fighting. So I signed up for rest and recuperation at home and a second tour.

I told my crew what I had chosen and recommended that they go home. They did, except for my bombardier. He, too, signed up for a second tour. Neither of us had time to discuss it or make a careful, rational choice.

After our meeting at Division Headquarters, we returned to find the base under restrictions. No one could leave, all liquor was forbidden, and no contact was allowed with anyone off the base. Briefings were going on. The invasion was imminent — probably on 6 June.

I could stand it no longer. On 5 June, I went to see my Squadron Commander and told him, "I want to fly in the invasion. I'll be most happy to consider it the first mission of my second tour."

He called Headquarters with my request; but they turned it down. The Commander suggested that if I wanted to help, I could line up planes in takeoff order. Because there were to be so many missions flown, the planes had to be in takeoff order on the taxiway. I helped, but it certainly was not the same as flying in the big show.

Throughout all this the weather had been the biggest obstacle. We were finally on the continent of Fortress Europe, and the end of the war was drawing closer. But many of the missions flown that night got mixed up. British Bomber Command and the 8th and 9th Air Forces were flying, but no one had coordinated the forming flares for the different commands. Our Group was to form on a lead, firing triple green flares. However, some British Halifaxes were also forming on triple green flares, and so were some 9th Air Force B-26s.

Those flying found little opposition in the air; everything turned out fine. I hated to have missed the show. We won the air offensive over Europe, and only a couple of German planes even got over the invasion area.

My bombardier, Art, and I said our good-byes to the crew. A day later we were at the port, boarding a ship for Boston and home. Our crew would follow when space was available. Those of us heading home received royal treatment.

Chapter 13

Thirty-five airmen climbed the gangplank of the luxury liner *Manhattan*, bound for the States. The interior of the ship had been burned out in Singapore, but, after a complete refurbishment, it again sailed, as the pride of the Coast Guard. She carried equipment and supplies needed to transport American troops to and from battle zones. Many German prisoners of war also were brought aboard, the first captured by U.S. forces following the invasion of the continent. The number of German prisoners who were Russian surprised me; they had Asiatic features. Many Russians apparently agreed to fight for the Germans. What a weird world we live in. So much made no sense.

The Captain aboard the *Manhattan* told us that a small Mess had been set up and that we could go in and order steak any time, day or night. The prisoners would receive adequate food, but not steak. Also on board the ship were USO entertainers, mostly comedians who lived in our area; they made the journey a really fun trip for us.

We did not sail in convoy because our ship could outrun any German submarines. The Germans could not intercept us because we were sailing with evasive action.

Art and another officer got up early and stood on the stairs when the prisoners marched to the Mess, forcing them to salute. But Art soon tired of getting up early.

I felt full, with something wanting release — as if I would explode if I could not get relief. I suddenly realized that I had not seen anything in color since I went into combat. I saw almost everything in black, white, and gray. The only other colors were the red and orange of bursting antiaircraft shells and the red flames of burning aircraft. It was weird. The sky was not blue; it was gray. Did I ever see the sun at all? I couldn't remember. The countryside, the people, trains, and planes were in black, white, and gray. Maybe that was how the mind functioned to keep our sanity.

When we docked in Boston Harbor, the Army rushed us by bus to Camp Miles Standish. They put us in tents and told us to wait. But we had not flown combat to spend our time in a tent city. We persuaded a couple of the ranking officers to see if they could get us out of there. They found another officer with the necessary authority, who agreed to help us. He got us orders for 30 days at home. We were to leave as a group and return as a group. The leave orders took travel time into account, so everyone would have the full 30 days with families and friends. Officers living in the east would thereby have an additional 10 days at home while others traveled.

We boarded the train in Providence for the trip to New York City that afternoon and arrived that evening. None of us knew where to go. A booth in the depot was staffed by volunteers acting as unofficial hostesses for servicemen. One of the volunteers looked at our orders. We told her we were on R and R and had 30 days' leave.

She said, "You mean you're just back from combat? This is your first day back in the United States?"

I said, "Yes, Ma'am. We don't know where to stay." She picked up the phone, and after a couple of calls, she said, "Go to the Hotel New Yorker."

Art, Captain Lothar, a B-26 driver, and I were given a suite fit for a king. It had a living room and bedrooms, and at no cost to us. That was some deal. We went to the suite and had a drink. Then we called our wives. Talking to Jeri was the highlight of the whole day. I told her I would be home shortly.

Later that evening we went to the Army Transportation Office in Grand Central Station to make reservations, but we were told that it might be several days before we'd get them. We were to go back in the morning.

We took in a stage show that night, then wandered around the city. One fact was obvious — people in the United States were oblivious to what the war was all about. It didn't affect them directly, so they remained unobservant to what war did to people, and they just went about their daily lives. But the war seemed to have been good for the unemployment problem.

At first light the next morning, we went back to the Transportation Office. We had no intention of spending another day in New York. It was eating into our allotted time. We tried all day to get a train reservation, but to no avail.

That evening, Lothar headed for Texas. Art and I simply climbed aboard a train bound for Chicago. Art was from Peoria, and he could make it the rest of

Chapter 13

the way home easily from there, but I would have to start the whole travel process again. We went into the vestibule and sat until the train was under way. Then we told the conductor that we had no seat or place to sleep. Though this made him angry, the train was already moving, so he finally agreed to let us stay in the rest room during the trip.

When we arrived in Chicago, I had to go to another depot to go west. A serviceman who used to work for the railroad said that if we could find 13 people traveling our way, we could get out of there. The railroad would have to add a car to handle 13 or more persons. We accomplished it more quickly than I had imagined possible; we petitioned for a car — which they added, probably because it was the path of least resistance.

Our car was no beauty; in fact, it was filthy. But it moved west as the rest of the train did, and that's all I wanted, to get home. My wife had told me on the phone that my parents would be coming to Seattle to see me. At about eight o'clock that night, we went through my hometown. I did not know it, but my folks had gotten on the second section of the train I was riding.

I arrived in Seattle about eight in the morning, and my wife was there to meet me. She had arranged to come alone to the station because we needed those first moments together. When we got home, all the relatives were there. The important thing was seeing my wife and boys. I couldn't believe how much my sons had grown.

Although I treasured my time at home, part of me was still back in the war and always would be. Jeri never criticized me for volunteering; she understood all my feelings. Although she may not have agreed, she understood, and we could live with that.

The visit at home was the first time that 30 days seemed less than a week. Time passed quickly and my leave ended. We didn't do much, other than spend the time together.

I had been smart enough to make an advance reservation for the return train trip. I was to meet Art in Chicago, and from there we would go to Atlantic City to the Redistribution Center where we would all assemble and return together.

One fact was obvious to me — most Americans were better off — more prosperous — in this time of war than they ever had been before. Even though everyone complained about rationing, it was a relatively minor inconvenience.

When I walked into the hotel in Atlantic City, my friend Bill Ross was sitting on the desk. I couldn't believe my eyes. His plane had gone down on New Year's Eve 1943. We began a real reunion then and there.

Bill's plane had received a few bad hits, and two crewmen had received wounds. They had no choice other than to bail out. The plane had crashed near them, but no Germans had appeared. Bill and the bombardier had gone down together, but the bombardier had been badly wounded. His parachute was swinging, and he had hit a stone wall. He had suffered several broken bones

The author visiting home in Kennewick, WA, in the summer of 1944.

Chapter 13

The Swayze family relaxing on a fishing trip at Twin Lakes, WA, in July 1944.

and a slight concussion.

The other surviving crewmen had taken off, hoping to evade the Germans. But Bill had stayed with the bombardier to give what aid he could. When he had looked up, a young French girl was standing there looking at them. She could speak some English. With that and sign language, she had let them know she would bring help and would not turn them over to the Germans.

The girl had returned with members of her family who had helped Bill and his bombardier to a dugout under their house where they constructed a bed. Bill and his bombardier stayed for several months while the bombardier's wounds healed. The French family had risked their lives to help. If the Germans had caught them aiding the enemy, they would have been executed.

One day while with the family, Bill and the bombardier were cutting each other's hair when they looked up and saw two German soldiers standing beside the fence, watching them. The Germans did not seem to realize they were American fliers. Bill and the bombardier had even gone to the local tavern with the Frenchman. They had sat there with Germans all around them and had a few glasses of wine.

In a few months they were well enough to join the underground and make their way to Spain. Bill found out later that the Germans had learned that the family had aided the Americans and had executed them.

Bill and his bombardier had climbed over the Pyrenees into Spain in the company of a fighter pilot. Once in Spain, they had turned themselves in. The Spanish had shaved their heads and put them in a jail that was infested with ticks, lice, and all sorts of vermin. The food was rotten, but they had eaten it to stay alive.

After a month in jail, the Spanish had allowed them to continue on to Gibraltar where they were under British control and were returned to England. From there they returned to the States where they had also just arrived at the Redistribution Center. What an experience they had endured.

It took three days for our group of 35 officers to reassemble. By that time the decision to return to combat looked less wise to me than when I had volunteered. We were moved to a port base in New Jersey where we waited to board a ship back to England. We remained there for three more days in relative isolation. Our only contact was with some Australian officers. They couldn't understand our restriction and loaned their uniforms to anyone in our group who could fit into them. Everyone but me went out on the town; I was too big to fit into any of the Australian uniforms!

By that time, Italy had surrendered and many former Italian soldiers were in the States. We had to treat them as our allies. That change was hard for me to swallow. They had gone from being an enemy trying to kill me to an ally I had to stand behind in the Mess line. I found that very difficult. Then when evening came, the Italians got into cars bearing New York plates driven by

Chapter 13

chauffeurs with good-looking girls inside. They went in to New York for fun and games. I was bitter because I couldn't even phone my wife. I'll never understand our politicians' decisions.

Three men in our group who had changed their minds about returning must have had political influence because they received new orders for assignments in the States. One of them who had filled his footlocker with bottles of bourbon for the crossing willed it to us. It would be some comfort on the trip back to England, we thought, as we boarded the *Queen Elizabeth*.

The major contingent on the ship was the 9th Armored Division. There were also about 500 Red Cross girls going overseas to work as hostesses and a group of nurses assigned to a field hospital, who added color to the voyage back. We received cabin assignments that mixed us in with Armored officers of our same rank, which led to a lot of friction. We had been issued the same combat gear as the Armored guys, which was ridiculous. We already had all of our gear at our bases in England. So most of our new gear "fell" overboard into the harbor.

Also as we boarded, we were each given a card with a number. Mine was a purple five. I soon found out what the number represented — I was to eat twice a day, at five in the morning and five in the afternoon. I learned not to miss those times or I went hungry.

Eating a British breakfast at five o'clock in the morning was a bit hard to take. It consisted of a couple of thick, half-cooked slices of bacon containing no lean at all, a bony white fish reminding me of carp, and a slab of hard bread with no butter or spread of any kind. I would soften the bread in the bacon grease or fish juice. I learned to hate a limey breakfast!

We thought British food was the worst in the world; the reputation was fitting and deserved. The evening meal consisted of Brussels sprouts, Spam or fish, and hard white bread, two inches thick. The beverage was a mug of coal black tea. If it had not been for the bourbon, I would have starved. No wonder the British fought so well and so hard. Their food would make anyone want to fight.

Our rooms contained a network of pipes forming frames about one foot apart. An oblong piece of canvas stretched between the frames. These were our bunks. The man above was so near that my nose touched the bottom of his canvas if I turned onto my back. That was closeness.

We hated the whole situation — a full schedule of air raid drills, boat drills, and athletic events. We jogged around the deck of the ship to stay in shape. But we decided we would not attend any formations. If our names were not on any list, we would not be marked absent from formation.

On the third day out, a Major came into our room and found us having a bourbon and water during boat drill. He acted as if we had just stolen all of the gold in Fort Knox. He posted us to appear before the Division Commander,

Major General Leonard, who decided to throw us to the wolves. He assigned us troop duty down in the lower decks.

My friend, the B-26 jockey, told General Leonard we couldn't accept that duty. He said our orders were for rest and recuperation. and that excluded troop duties. I couldn't believe it! The General dismissed us, saying that he would get back to us, but he never did. And we didn't attend any more activities than we had before.

The case of bourbon and the five-day trip ended at about the same time. Major Gill, a field grade officer who was in charge of our group, had told us to let him know when we wanted to go up to the lounge. He could ride on the elevator; the rest of us were company grade and normally had to use the stairs. But when we would go to the lounge, he would bluff a ride for us on the elevator, claiming we were his guests. It worked.

When we reached Southampton, we boarded trains to our various outfits. Art and I arrived at the small railroad station about five miles from our field, but no one was there to meet us. I called our base; it was a couple of hours before a truck arrived to pick us up.

We had not expected a big welcome, but we did not appreciate standing on the depot platform for so long. We didn't know which squadron we would be in. We signed in at the Visiting Officers Quarters and went to the Club. The evening meal was already over, and the next one would be the midnight meal for the fliers, so we decided to have a few drinks.

There were a dozen or so officers drinking in the Club, but no one we knew. We started talking to them anyway, and everyone we asked about had either rotated or had been shot down. It was a blow. I had returned to the war to stand by my friends. None remained. Even the Squadron Commander was new. My favorite Squadron Commander had gone down and was a prisoner of war.

The crew members we talked to were hostile toward us, as if they feared that we might break up their crews. We represented something new, and they became suspicious automatically. This disillusioned me. Why had I returned? I should have known I could not go back to find that nothing had changed. It was not possible. All the same, it was unsettling.

I went about getting loaded and was doing a pretty good job. I went to the rest room to recycle the beer. Art came in with one eye closed and a trickle of blood running down his face. He said, "They hit me. Help me."

There was nothing to do but come out swinging. I knocked down the officer who had hit Art. Then I kicked him hard enough to take the heel off of one of my GI boots. I dived into a Major, and hurt him. I decided it was time to leave. I found my boot heel, went back to my quarters, cleaned up, and put on another pair of boots.

By that time, they were serving the midnight meal, so I went to eat. The Group Commander who had tried to court-martial me was the only officer

Jack Swayze receiving his first Distinguished Flying Cross after his first tour, 1944.

there that I knew; he got into line with me. I had filled my tray and sat down when I noticed he had not taken any food. He followed along, sat down next to me, and said, "I didn't want you back here. You've put a couple of crew members in the hospital and have broken the ribs of the Supply Squadron Commander. You may choose to stay in the Air Corps the rest of your life, but I'll see that you never make Captain." With that, he got up and left. My welcome was complete!

I found out a couple of days later that the injuries were not that serious. No one held any grudges. It was just one of those events of wartime. We eventually became good friends. And the threat to prevent my promotion was empty. I received my Distinguished Flying Cross and promotion to Captain the following week.

The next morning I went to meet my Squadron Commander, Lieutenant Colonel John Grable. I liked him on sight. He said that he had not received any assignment for me or my bombardier. Fliers usually came as complete crews, so we were a problem. He said he didn't know what Headquarters had in mind for returnees. There were no staff positions open. He said my bombardier could work with the Squadron bombardier and that I could hang around with him. And that was what we did.

I got up in the mornings and went with John to mission briefing. Then we went back to his quarters. When it was time for the planes to return, we went to the line and watched them come back, put in for replacement crews and aircraft, and checked the next mission. We went to the Club after that and had a few drinks until it was time to turn in. John and I became good friends; we saw this war business the same way.

We were in his jeep one day, going to meet the incoming crews, when the Group Commander stopped him; they engaged in a lengthy conversation. I had a hunch that I was the topic. When John came back, he said, "You'll start flying again."

A crew with only two missions had gone down in France, evaded the enemy, and made it into friendly territory. The Crew Commander didn't want to fly anymore; his crew had not liked him. My bombardier and I would take over that crew.

John told me, "You'll be getting a new Squadron Commander. Our Group Operations Officer got promoted to full Colonel and is moving to Division Headquarters. So I'm moving up to Group Operations. We're also getting a new Group Commander. He'll arrive soon."

Chapter 14

When I finally met my new crew, I saw at once the reason they had failed; they lacked discipline. We were to fly locally, develop our procedures, and then go on a mission. I had told them to be at the plane at a specific time, but they did not show up. I found them asleep on a pile of flight suits. As a result, we had a "come-to-Jesus meeting." I put the engineer, the ranking NCO, in charge. I gave him detailed instructions on how we would function as a crew and told him that I held him responsible for enlisted crew members. He would report directly to me. I told him, "You've used up one of your allotted three strikes. I'll take action if this crew makes another mistake."

We were to fly a mission the next day, and once again the crew failed to show up at the plane on time. I made it clear once more to the engineer and the rest of the crew that three strikes and they would be out.

Our first mission was on 27 August to Oranienburg, located northeast of Berlin. During my first tour, I had vowed to change the way I climbed to altitude to join the Group. On the 27th I chose to try my new method. I climbed over the Channel, proceeded to Control Point "A," and circled, waiting for our Group to arrive. The weather was horrible. We were near 26,000 feet before we broke out on top of the undercast. It surprised me to find ten other B-24s, from different Groups, doing what I was doing. Maybe this method of climbing was as dangerous as the race-track course!

The time came to leave for Control Point "B" near the Jutland Peninsula.

All of us took off in a gaggle. As we approached the Peninsula, we saw a bunch of German FW-190s up ahead, high and coming our way. A tight formation formed in a hurry. I managed to get the lead of the bucket element, a favorite position of mine. There were about 50 German fighters. They came from the front, rolled over, and flew through our formation upside down, exposing only their underside which was protected by an armor plate; we could do little damage to them.

They performed the strangest maneuver. As they went through our formation firing, they did a "Split S," and disappeared. They passed so closely that we could see their faces and hair color. One in particular surprised me — he had bright red hair. This one wave of FW-190s shot down five of our B-24s. If they had stayed around, they probably could have gotten us all. But they didn't; they must have been low on fuel.

We moved into a six-ship box. Art didn't have the information he needed for us to drop on our own. We knew the lead ship was from the 44th and was carrying general-purpose 500-pound bombs. His number two aircraft was from the 93rd, and it was also carrying general-purpose bombs, although they were 1,000-pounders. The other planes, according to the field order, were heading for the same target we were — an aircraft factory.

Art decided that I should watch the bombs drop from the lead, count to six, and then call "bombs away." The delay in dropping should put our incendiary bombs right on target. We had a K-24 camera mounted in the waist and would have a full photo story of the bombing results. I watched the bombs come out of the lead, dutifully counted to six, and then gave my call. The lead ship's bombs hit short of the factory area. Our incendiaries spread in a pattern over the buildings, and fires began to climb skyward. We turned southwest toward Berlin, flew just north of the city, and crossed over Dumar Lake. The German Abbeyville Kids flew from this area. But no one came up to challenge us, which was a surprise. The Germans put up some flak, but we didn't see a single German fighter all the way home to England.

Crossing the Channel, we broke off to our respective bases. England was shrouded in a blanket of fog and clouds, and we had trouble locating our field. When we finally found it, there were unfamiliar planes parked all over. I called for landing, received clearance, and put down. We taxied to a set hardstand. When I called for transportation, the tower said we would have to walk in. I asked, "Who is the tower officer?"

"This is Lieutenant Colonel Webb," he said. "After flying lost all day over England, you can walk in."

I was angry and replied, "We're back from a combat strike. We have pictures to prove it. If you'll come get the film and develop it, you'll see that we hit the target." That set him back. A truck soon arrived. I prayed as we rode to debriefing that we did have good pictures. They were, and we were

Chapter 14

vindicated. It seemed that a recall of the mission had been broadcast, but we had not heard it because we were too far out over the Channel. I decided then to return to the normal race-track method of climbing so that this wouldn't happen again. Our Group put in for and received credit for participation in the mission.

The crew, except for Art and the copilot, still showed a genuine lack of desire and discipline. I knew we could not survive with them, so I made an appointment to see my new Squadron Commander, Lieutenant Colonel Stroud. He was understanding. He agreed with me and said he would assign them to the defensive guns around the base to give them time to think and hopefully decide to follow orders. He said there was an engineer just back from the hospital recovering from wounds who wanted to finish his tour and could join us. The Commander sent for him, a Technical Sergeant, a native of Texas. When he arrived, I could simply tell by his appearance that he was a superior young man. He knew my reputation, and we hit it right off. He asked who we would get for the rest of the crew, and I suggested he pick out the men he wanted, give me their names, and I would get them assigned.

He did, and we put together a good crew. I retained the officers from my old crew, and we were ready to do some flying. For the first time since returning, I believed we could fly successful missions. I was once again a happy warrior. Colonel Stroud wisely suggested that we fly locally for a couple of weeks to whip procedures into shape, so we did. The more I flew with those guys, the more I liked them. They were good. The engineer had picked from among wounded men who wanted to finish their tours. And my experience completing a tour gave them confidence in me as a pilot.

On 18 September we briefed to fly to Groesbeek, Holland. The Army had tried to take the bridges over the Rhine at Arnhem, but the whole operation was snake-bit. The 101st and the 82nd Airborne Divisions were in deep trouble; they needed to be resupplied or the Germans would wipe them out. Headquarters had tried a resupply with C-47s on 17 September but had taken severe losses and thus had decided to call on the B-24s.

We flew nine abreast and as low as possible. Panels on the ground marked our drop area. After completing the drop, we were to climb to 1,500 feet and make a climbing turn for home. All possible supplies had been loaded in the bomb bay. In the waist, more had been piled, which we would drop through the camera hatch. An Army Private would ride in the waist and help with the drop. He would join an Army unit on the ground if we crashed.

We crossed the Holland coast on the deck and flew across the dikes and the countryside, not flying an inch higher than was necessary to clear the terrain. It was quite a sight. There were German vehicles trying to get out of the way, and Germans on the dikes and buildings firing at us with small arms. Mobile antiaircraft guns now and then also shot at us from the side. Those directly below us didn't have much of a chance to hit us.

The Dutch people were something to see. They were in yards and on buildings, waving at us with flags and articles of clothing. We could see how much they were willing to risk to show us their support.

When we reached the target, we pulled up and dropped. I should have climbed out immediately, but I enjoyed seeing the natives. So I leveled out and kept watching. It was a real highlight.

Other planes began to call and complain because we were not climbing and they were getting hit. My engineer came down out of the turret and showed me a ring of bullet holes in my side window. There were seven holes from rounds that should have hit me. That did it. Reality came back to me quickly, and I went into a climb. We got out of there fast. Those first two missions had been so emotional that I had not had time to realize I was back in the war.

Our Division lost four bombers. One B-24 flew too low and hit a dike, bending over the props on all engines about four inches. However, he still made it back to England for an emergency landing.

Shortly after that flight, Colonel Stroud called for me to report. I feared he was going to take me apart for not climbing, but that was not the case. He said, "We're going to have our own lead crews for bombing in bad weather. We'll be receiving planes equipped with radar to give us the capability to bomb in or through an overcast. We'll have a Mickey Operator (navigator) assigned for each mission. Selected crews will stand down and fly daily practice over England. Your crew is one of them. Will you do this?" I assured him we would.

Immediately I loved the radar system's capability and the accuracy with which the operator could read the scope. Flying straight and level on a long bomb run worried me, though. I had stayed alive by using evasive action, but none was possible on a 40- to 80-mile-long bomb run, because we were using the Pathfinder radar bombing system.

Our baptism came on 2 October when we flew deputy lead on a mission to Hamm, Germany. The long run was torture. There was a steady barrage of flak throughout. I watched for a few minutes, then scooted down in the seat and watched the instruments. Out of the corners of my eyes, I could see the bursts all around us. I was happy to still be in one piece when it was time for "bombs away." I did some serious praying on that long run.

The next day, 3 October, we were scheduled to go to Pforzheim, Germany. I was deputy lead and could, if the flight was not a visual, take over the run. At briefing, our new Group Commander, Colonel Westover, spoke. He knew that personnel of the Group were unhappy about not having a Presidential Unit Citation. But he said, "Decorations are nothing more than hardship ribbons." The Colonel felt that decorations too often proved someone had messed up or had blundered into something tough and had to fight his way out. The leader of a mission may well deserve a court-martial, he said, but evidence often does not exist, nor would it accomplish anything if it did. And the result, the Colonel added, is a disastrous mission, and an award gets presented. He said, "Today's is a perfect mission for you to get a Presidential Unit Citation. I'll tell you how to do it."

He told us the crews were to decide which would go down. Then he said, "Those returning will receive the Citation. I can guarantee it. Now, you decide whether you want a Citation or a good mission. I trust you choose a good mission and help to bring this war to an end."

I had never been in a quieter briefing room or seen a group of men more impressed. We knew that this was a Commander to go the route with. We flew a good mission, had good bomb results, and kept casualties low. No one mentioned a Presidential Unit Citation again.

We flew to Clausthal K in Germany on 7 October. It was another good mission, and everything went very well. So far, no man flying with me had been injured, nor had I lost a plane on any mission I had led.

At about this time, Headquarters came up with a new rule for staff officers. Each had to fly five missions as a crew member or spare man. It seemed silly. And because staff personnel did not believe I would be shot down, I had at least 14 men on board each mission. We flew as usual and said nothing, hoping the war would end soon.

One crew told us of having been to the emergency strip at Manston where they had seen British planes flying faster than anything the rest of the Allies owned. They were chasing buzz bombs and flew without propellers. So, after dropping practice bombs one afternoon, we then flew to Manston to see for ourselves. We landed on the runway without calling in. And sure enough, parked on hardstands in the trees stood these strange-looking fighters. They were British Meteors. After seeing them, we had a better idea what it was that the Germans had that were passing by us so fast; they were ME-262 jets and ME-163 rocket planes. We realized that if we did not win this war quickly, we could see it turn in Germany's favor. The Meteors proved that someone on our side was with the program and developing new aircraft for the Allies, too.

V-1 "flying bomb" attacks on London had become routine, but the newer V-2 rocket was striking terror into the British. We could defend against the V-1. There was no defense against the V-2.

We flew on a raid to Koblenz, Germany, on 9 October. It was a fairly routine mission, and there was no sign of the mighty Luftwaffe. It was not that the Luftwaffe was any less of a force, but we were flying more bombers daily, and more fighters were escorting us, covering us all the way. This took a heavy toll on German fighters. The Germans could not hit all of us. They did, however, install more and bigger flak guns and, in turn, took a toll on American bombers.

On 14 October, we flew to Cologne, Germany, and once again it was a fairly routine show. Cologne and Koblenz got hit more than any other German cities. The cathedrals were primary targets, secondary targets, and targets of opportunity. Yet through it all, they stood. My personal feeling was that no one could witness that and question whether there was a God. Hitler's works crumbled, while God's remained intact. What a lesson for the German people.

Between mid-October and 10 November, we trained with the new Pathfinder radar. We flew with both a visual and a radar lead. We bombed visually, unless weather prevented it. We had radar leads doing both jobs. If we could not bomb visually, we could do the job by using radar. We had enough planes on hand to support the increased operations. We heard there were enough bombers stockpiled in England to support any losses. We could lose all of the 8th Air Force on three consecutive days and still put up a full force on the fourth day. We didn't have that many crews, but we had the planes.

On 10 November, we led, and a friend from our Group Operations was flying copilot. We had learned at briefing that our Group Commander, Colonel Westover, would fly with us as Command Pilot. He would meet us at the plane.

The target was a single-track railroad east of Frankfurt, Germany. Art questioned the target; he didn't believe Headquarters would send that many bombers to hit a single-track railroad, nor attack a target with the bomb run crossing a major target such as Frankfurt. When he raised the question, the briefer said, "Shut up and go where briefed."

We got to the plane, ran the normal checks, and climbed on board. We had to wait until it was time to start the engines, and I told Bruce not to offer his copilot seat to the Commander, nor would I. We didn't know his capabilities — how he'd perform in combat. All the while we were talking, someone was standing between us. I assumed it was our engineer, awaiting the order to start the "putt-putt" for power to start the engines. When it was time, I turned to tell the engineer to start it and looked right at a pair of eagles. I stammered, "I thought you were our engineer."

He said, "Think nothing of it. I would not take one of your seats anyway."

I wished that incident had not happened. The Commander was actually a superior officer and went on to become Commanding General of Air Defense Command.

On approach to Frankfurt that day, Art called me, wanting to hit the marshaling yard at Frankfurt. I called the Colonel and put it up to him. He said, "I will not order a lead crew. I will advise only. If you go where briefed and something goes wrong, I can help you. If you go off on your own and something goes wrong, there is nothing I can or will do to help."

That made sense. I called the other Groups and told them to go where we went and bomb where we did. There were 300 to 400 bombers on that raid,

Chapter 14

and only three bombs hit the railroad. It was a single-track line, never completed or connected to anything.

After we had landed and taxied to the hardstand, I learned that there was a problem. A staff car with a General's star was waiting.

When I climbed down, the General asked, "Are you the pilot?" I said, "Yes, Sir, but the Colonel is on board." By that time, Colonel Westover had come out. He reported to General Timberlake, and they drove off.

I thought, "Someone's in trouble. I hope not us." We went to the debriefing. A major I did not know sat in and listened to all we said without uttering a word. Then he took all of our paperwork and the mission folder and left.

We found out that night that someone in Intelligence had misread the target coordinates. The target *should* have been the marshaling yard in Frankfurt that Art had wanted to bomb. Our Group Intelligence soon had many new faces.

That night in the Club, General Timberlake asked to see my hat. He said, "That's the most battered hat I have seen."

I told him, "My hat has made every mission with me sitting on it. It's good luck. We'd all be afraid to fly without me on it. When this war ends, I might give it to you, but not now." He implied that I should get a new one, but I didn't. My crew and I held on to our superstition.

We hit Bielefeld, Germany, on 26 November and attended the usual critique that night. Lead crews sat in front. As usual, we did not remove our caps. We went over the mission, looking for ways to improve. This provided the staff with the information needed to make their reports to higher Headquarters.

When the Colonel arrived, he said, "It's time to restore some military courtesy to these meetings. All personnel should remove their caps and stand at attention when the Commander enters." I didn't look around to see what the others had done. The Colonel then said, "This applies to everyone but old slaphappy here. Don't pay any attention to him. He doesn't know any better." I looked around. I was the only one who had not removed his cap. I did so from then on.

Chapter 15

The 8th Air Force sent its bombers to raid Neunkirchen, Germany, on 30 November. The Allied ground advance was eating up Europe in chunks. We believed it was all over but the shouting; the Third Reich was sinking fast. Morale was high and mission results were good.

My crew and I flew deputy lead, and we were returning home with only slight damage. We passed over flak batteries that put their bursts directly between our ship and the lead ship. I evaded to the right, but the bursts followed our plane, coming ever closer. I knew beyond any doubt that they had their radar locked on us. We were trying to save ourselves by flying an ever-increasing bank in turns to the right and left, but those Germans were not about to give up. The bursts had our names written on them. The large orange centers told me they were much too close; we were getting shrapnel hits. It sounded like someone throwing a bucket of gravel at the side of a steel building.

I knew I had to do more, or they were going to nail us. I called our lead — "I'll be breaking formation for a bit" — then went into a steep turn to the north. I increased the bank until the wings were past vertical, then rolled back into a burst, increasing the bank as we returned to course. The Germans's lock on us held in spite of my evasive action. The bursts were getting still closer. I had no choice. I went into a maximum climb and gained at least 5,000 feet. Evasive action and the climb loosened the aircraft. I then descended, making wild turns. The flak battery began losing us to distance, and I got back into position in our formation. It was the closest we had come to getting shot down by a flak battery. Those Germans had to be a first-line bunch; they knew what they were doing. We were lucky. If they had crippled us with their opening shots, we would have been theirs.

Next we hit the supply depot at Hanau, Germany, on 11 December. We made our bomb run from the north, and all of our Group's bombs were on the target area. I still did not like the long, straight bomb runs. But by then we were doing more evasive maneuvers because our navigator and bombardier began coordinating their actions. They could work with each other and make evasive turns on the bomb run. Those turns made a big difference in controlling flak damage.

After bombs away, we were to make a maximum turn away from the target, descending 1,000 feet and slowing 10 miles per hour. That was the procedure for all of the 8th Air Force. I decided to be different. I would climb 1,000 feet and *increase* our speed 10 miles per hour. The reason for the original procedure had been to make it easier for stragglers. I figured the Germans knew what we were doing and would expect the same action from all Groups, so our doing the opposite would confuse them. When I climbed and increased speed, we got out of the flak at once. I could see it coming up to our right a couple of thousand feet below us. It tickled me to see the German gunners fall into the trap. I didn't know how long we could get away with it, but it beat staying in the flak barrage.

We landed to the news of the German advance in the Battle of the Bulge. The Germans had worn American uniforms in weather made to order for them. It looked like they might cut Allied armies in half and make it all the way to the sea. This was serious business. The Allies were in a world of hurt. A pea-soup fog covered the low countries, stopping all air support, at a time when the need for it had increased.

We flew on 19 December to support our forces in the Bulge. Headquarters was gambling on a break in the weather. It had set up instrument-landing-system equipment to create a line past which it was safe to drop: when the needle was in the yellow.

The weather finally eased, and we made a good drop on German positions in the Ehrang area. The bombing helped stop the German advance. With the improved weather, 8th and 9th Air Force fighters began to tear up the Nazi forces. They found and destroyed the German armor spearheading the advance.

On 28 December, we flew on a raid to Kaiserslautern. There was heavy flak in the target area, and we took some hits, though I thought damage to our plane was not too serious. Coming off the target, however, the oil pressure started to drop on our number four engine. I feathered it at once, thinking that would solve the problem. About ten minutes later, the number three engine had rising oil and cylinder-head temperatures. The oil pressure was dropping, the rpm was erratic, and the manifold pressure was oscillating. There was no choice but to feather number three and drop out of formation.

I knew that the British had three fields in the area. The weather was a solid undercast, and the Mickey Operator said he could pick up Brussels. Trying to make it across the Channel with two engines down didn't appear to be a viable solution, so we headed for Brussels on our own. I went over the situation with the engineer. Because I had feathered number four early, it might restart to give us power for landing.

The weather report said the ceiling around Brussels was 1,000 feet, and visibility was 3 miles. My plan was to call Brussels and secure landing clearance. The Mickey Operator would bring us over the city's center as we descended to 1,000 feet. We should be able to find the proper field without any problem. I didn't realize it, but complacency had become a factor affecting my judgment. I called Brussels approach control for clearance to land and was told, "Clear to land using Runway 28, call on downwind leg."

I briefed the crew. We descended without new problems. I decided to unfeather number four at 1,500 feet while we were still in the soup. Number four unfeathered, and I tried to start it, but it wouldn't run. I tried several times. We dropped below 1,000 feet, and I spotted the field off to our right about 10 miles away. I hit the feathering button for number four to refeather and reduce the drag, but it wouldn't feather. Now I had ripped it. We were hurting with two engines feathered on one side. With one windmilling and one feathered, I was in real trouble. It was likely that the windmilling engine would freeze from oil starvation. I was in dire straits. This was an emergency, and I would have only one shot at landing.

Calling the tower, I declared our emergency and requested that they clear all traffic. We flew a short downwind leg. There was a Gooney Bird — a C-47 — in front of us. I asked the tower to have them pull out of the way. The tower did, but the Gooney didn't answer, nor did the pilot try to clear our path. I wasn't going to crash to miss him. I was going on in, hoping I could stay behind him. I slowed down as much as I dared, praying he would not go to full power. That would have left us in the prop wash. I knew control would be critical when I reduced power on engines one and two.

Coming down final, I was gaining on the Gooney, and the outcome was in doubt. I believe the good Lord stepped in, and the Gooney Bird landed long down the runway. I touched down on the first 10 feet. It had been foolish to unfeather number four engine. I would never make that mistake again.

We could not taxi off the runway with two engines out on one side, so we sat until we got a tow. They parked us in a line of broken-down B-17s and B-24s. By the time I reached Operations, the Gooney Bird crew had left. That probably saved me more problems, for I was as angry as I had ever been.

We were quartered in a schoolhouse in the outskirts of Brussels. We didn't know if we could have repairs made to our bird; all we could do was wait and see. We dropped into a small local bar that night, having rounded up enough money for a few beers. An elderly gentleman in the bar became fascinated by the shoes my engineer was wearing. He had on a heated suit, and the high-top electric boots covered his legs and feet. It looked as if he had immense feet because the heated shoes fit over his GI boots.

This gentleman came back the next night with his wife. They bent over to look at my engineer's boots. But we decided it would be a crime to tell them his feet were not actually that large.

The young woman tending bar asked if we had been on the raid bombing the marshaling yard. We said that we had, and she told us that her father had died in that raid. He had operated a switch engine for the railroad. I could remember the engines and cars looking like toys being thrown into the air and then exploding. I was sorry we had admitted taking part, though she displayed good will, not anger, toward us. I thought perhaps that I might not have been as understanding. But the people of Belgium wanted the Germans out so badly, they accepted their own losses.

On New Year's morning 1945, I awoke to the sound of aircraft flying. I could tell that they were not ours. I got up, looked out a window, and saw German fighters making passes across the airfield. Smoke was boiling up. A lot of damage was taking place. I didn't see any American or British fighters in the air. The Germans didn't stay long before heading back. I dressed and went out to the field; there was no use waiting any longer for repairs to our plane. All that remained of the row of bombers was a long line of black marks. Only scorched earth showed where our proud aircraft had stood.

I went to Operations to learn what I could. We were to be put on the first available flight back to England. About ten o'clock that morning, we boarded a C-47. The pilot was a service pilot who was privately trained and not Army Air Forces. I told him I wanted to fly in the copilot's seat. At first he refused, but finally he agreed. There was only the pilot and an engineer in the crew. He cranked up and we took off. He leveled out below a layer of broken clouds at about 200 feet; it was as rough as a cob. I knew it would be smoother up on top at 4,000 or 5,000 feet, so I said, "Why don't we go up on top of this stuff?" He answered that he couldn't fly instrument conditions, so we had to stay down there on VFR.

There wasn't much left to do but pray. We crossed the coast and flew over the Channel; it got rougher. After we were out of sight of land, his engineer reported one gear and the opposite flap were partway down. It was a dangerous condition, especially in rough air at less than 200 feet above the water. I became alarmed. Being in the copilot's seat was no help. I didn't know the Gooney Bird, but what little I had seen of it did not hearten me.

We were about halfway across the Channel so there was no point in turning back. Our destination was the emergency strip at Manston. For the next half hour, all I could do was sweat. Up ahead, we could see the coast. Then the left engine's instruments began to oscillate; we were losing it. I thought the plane had labored to fly on two engines and feared that trying to make it in on one would put us in the Channel. The pilot feathered number one and put full power on number two. We still could not hold altitude.

I radioed Manston for a straight-in approach and declared an emergency. The wind was from the north at about 40 knots. We were going to land with a crosswind. It took full power to stretch our descent to the field. We touched down, and the pilot tried to reduce power on number two. He couldn't hold the plane straight. A Gooney Bird normally didn't require much runway length, but he ran the full three miles and off into the overrun. Neither the plane nor the pilot impressed me.

Maintenance at Manston towed us in. They said they would change our engine at once so that we could continue in the morning. I was told in Operations that those people had to deliver us to our home base. I didn't like it.

We slept the night on cots in a tent and filed for Seething in the morning. We got in, started the engines, began to taxi, and a tire blew. That did it. I went into Operations and put in a call to our base for Lieutenant Colonel Grable in Group Operations. When I finally got him on the phone, I said, "This is Swayze. We're here at Manston. I beg you to send someone down in a B-24 and fly us back. Otherwise, we'll never make it."

He said, "Get something to eat. I'll pick you up in about two hours."

He arrived with only a navigator and a crew chief. When we were ready for takeoff, he said, "Have you ever tried taking off with two engines feathered?"

I said, "No, I haven't. This is a good place to try since it's three miles long."

He feathered numbers one and four and instructed me to start them up if we were not airborne within one mile. We almost had enough speed at that point, but the aircraft wouldn't fly. I unfeathered number one, started it, and we got off. I unfeathered number four and started it after we were airborne. I never enjoyed a flight more. It was a real pleasure to be on top in smooth air with four fans running.

John brought me up to date on what he knew of the war. Had the Germans succeeded at the Bulge, they could have split the First Army from the other Allied forces. Then, over time, they would have decimated the forces to the north. But the Germans hadn't succeeded. They had lost the forces Hitler would need to defend Germany proper. Instead, General Bradley had his First Army forces backed by General Patton to the south. Patton had made a forced march over 100 miles north to aid Bradley, leaving very weakened forces to the south.

Chapter 15

By then we knew that Germany was working on a nuclear bomb. The Allies believed that the Peenemünde raid had destroyed equipment and scientists and that the Germans would not have the new bomb in time to get the Americans out of England, but it would be close. We knew if the Germans started full production of the Messerschmitt 262, the Allies would be in difficulty. The same was true if they produced their Heinkel or Messerschmitt rocket planes. The 8th Air Force had nothing to match the performance of those planes. It was a race against time. The Allies had not counted on the mistakes Hitler made; still no sensible Commander would rely on mistakes made by his enemy to win.

About this time our forces in the Pacific were moving north toward the home island of Japan, but at immense cost. Priority had gone to the European Theater for men, weapons, and supplies.

As 1944 had come to a close, we had been optimistic. Yet we knew there was much more fighting to be done before victory. One bright spot was the new crews we were receiving. At the start, each Squadron in our Group had 18 crews. At the peak of the fighting for air control over Germany, we had dropped to 8. Finally we had 25 crews in each Squadron — the top crew status for the war. And we knew about that surplus of bombers in reserve in depots in England.

The more I flew, the more I saw and realized what could happen to us. But also the more I flew, the more I knew; and that made me better able to take care of the contingencies. Personally, I began to feel more pressure with every mission. Could I fly a few more successful ones? Would our luck as a crew hold? I knew we were flying better than ever, we had learned much, and we could take care of ourselves far better than we had in our early days. I also knew most of the bullets and flak were just "to whom it may concern." Could we avoid them?

Already there was talk of our going home. With the posting of who would fly with whom on what airplane, the pressure was rising, not dissipating, as we neared completion of our tours.

The nature of war had become ever more apparent as time went by. Although war is the most personal activity a man can participate in, it is highly impersonal. I know that seems to make very little sense, but it is true nonetheless. No one gets used to war. You may learn to control your fear, but only a total idiot could experience war without it; everyone is afraid. The main difference among men in war is the ability each has to control that fear. I felt that controlling my fear was my top personal achievement stemming from the war; I had learned to control it as well as any man. I had as much fear as anyone, but if I had anything going for me, it was my ability to understand it and do my job.

I also felt that I had earned my right to be a total citizen of this country of ours. I would never have to back up to the pay table, ever. Only those who have successfully faced combat understand this. War is destruction, brutality, and killing. There is nothing you do in war that builds, creates, or benefits man. All that you have when it's over is the knowledge that you controlled your fear and did all that your country asked.

Chapter 16

The Germans had launched V-2 rockets at England, especially London, in increasing numbers. The rocket, as a weapon system, pointed out the changes that would come in fighting future wars.

We were in London in early January 1945 on a three-day pass when a V-2 hit the entrance to the Regent Palace Hotel. The amount of damage impressed me — the ease with which the mission was accomplished impressed me even more.

My first personal observation of V-2 performance came soon after we had returned from London. We were waiting to board our plane and start engines for a raid into the heart of Germany. The Germans launched a V-2 from central Germany. It was a beautiful morning, with one of those rare clear-blue winter skies. The rocket left a persistent contrail, showing its flight path from beginning to end. We watched it rise, reach its zenith, and descend on London. Watching that flight made me realize I was also watching history unfold. The V-2 did not need a crew, and the mission lasted only five minutes.

About two weeks later, we had an overcast at about 2,000 feet. A V-2 came out of the murk and hit about half a mile off the end of our runway. It traveled at a speed we had never seen before. The explosion rocked the ground all around us. There was no doubt the rocket was going to replace the airplane as the delivery machine for weapons of war. I knew we had witnessed the future, and I wanted to get into the air and end the war before they blew us out of England.

Dropping bombs on Germany in 1945.

Chapter 16

Over Germany, 1945.

We knew that the Germans were working on a nuclear bomb, though at that time we had no idea of the power of that bomb much less that of a hydrogen bomb. But if Germany succeeded in developing and producing nuclear bombs, it could win the war. If it could deliver them on these rockets, we would certainly lose.

We did not know that the United States was racing to perfect its own nuclear bomb. Aircraft would be used to deliver the first. Later we would use our rockets to deliver them. To me the use of rockets seemed the only way to go. The V-1s had been vulnerable and easy to destroy in flight. But the V-2 was untouchable by any defense known to us at the time.

Historically, I suppose, the development of nuclear weapons is but another leap forward no greater than the leap from bows and arrows to gunpowder and guns. It takes a long time for nations to adopt new weapons. But as soon as they go into use, then the battle is on between the offense and the defense. First one and then the other has the advantage.

On 15 January we flew a mission to Kilchberg, Germany. There were no serious problems, and we had excellent bomb results. We flew a long haul to Dresden the next day. It was a tough mission. The flak was heavy, and ME-109s hit us as we were leaving the target. Our P-51s soon ran them off, but not before we lost a few planes and suffered serious damage to others.

We flew lead on a mission to Dortmund in the Ruhr on 28 January. We knew it was not going to be a picnic. At the briefing, our Group Commander introduced me to a Major from the Air Training Command and told me to see that he got checked out in Command radio procedures. He would be the Acting Command Pilot handling the radio calls to the other Groups.

Our Group would be the third Group back in the bomber stream and the third to bomb. At the briefing, I couldn't believe they had us flying down the bomb run at 18,000 feet. That was the worst altitude anyone could fly over the Ruhr. The German flak was extremely accurate at that altitude. My bombardier objected, along with the rest of the crew. For this mission we had drawn a different radar navigator, one who had a reputation for making excuses just before takeoff to avoid flying. I was not happy. When it was time to start engines, the Mickey Operator said, "Sir, I have to go to the bathroom."

I said, "I've heard about you. Forget it. We're taking off on time."

We had just begun to climb when other crewmen called to say they had to go. Our bomb bay would be a mess. It was too late, because we were already in the air and on our way.

An unpleasant feeling hit me at about 10,000 feet. By the time we reached 20,000 feet, I couldn't wait any longer. I made a dash for the bomb bay, but I didn't make it. I got back into my seat, sitting in what felt like a gallon of smelly liquid. The odor was something, even wearing an oxygen mask.

We received a call from the tower. Only half of the crews had taken off

Chapter 16

because of an epidemic of diarrhea.

When we were well over the continent, I called Art: "Are you ready to bomb at a higher altitude?" We talked it over and decided to bomb from 24,000 feet.

The new Major handling the radio said, "I've heard about you guys, how you don't follow the field order. If you vary from it by so much as a foot, I'll file charges." I argued without success. We dared not do anything other than fly at 18,000 feet.

When we turned on the bomb run, the Groups ahead were so high above us they resembled toys. I watched one Group about halfway down the bomb run. Three planes took hits, and two burst into flames and blew up. One trailed smoke and spiraled downward, disappearing into the murk below. I pointed this out to the Major, but he was oblivious. I told him we would never make it to the target. We were about halfway down the bomb run when a flak battery fired. All four shells hit our ship. A burst blew in through the side next to the copilot, and he landed between our seats. Another hit above the flight deck and took out part of the track of the top turret. Engines two and four had damage and were running at partial power. The manifold pressure on all four engines decreased, and we were down to 13,000 feet by the time I could get the engines controlled.

I kept calling my copilot's name. He didn't answer and acted as if he could hear nothing. He was reaching inside his shirt, pulling out his hand, and looking at it. He was wearing a flak vest, and it had saved his life.

He finally said, "I'm fine. My chest is full of holes. I'm all bloody." His chest turned black and blue, but what he thought was blood was only perspiration. The rest of the crew answered they were all fine.

I contacted Ground Sector Control and asked for a fix and steer to the nearest 9th Air Force fighter strip. We were low enough by then to see a small town below. I had to lift a wing over a church steeple. Then Control told us there was a fighter strip five minutes ahead. It was snowing lightly, and a couple of feet had collected on the ground. I couldn't see the PSP landing mat and kicked up a cloud of snow when I landed off of it. All went well, and we taxied to the appointed parking area. Once parked, we went to Operations. I tried to explain why I needed a shower, but a Brigadier General there said, "You'll fill out these papers first."

After the paperwork was completed, we were released to find a shower. My flight suit, jacket, and shoes were the only clothing I could salvage; the rest was beyond redemption. I burned them all in the furnace that heated the shower.

We later boarded a six-by-six truck and drove to Brussels. Once again we were to return to England on a C-47. But this time the bird had a military crew and all went fine on the trip.

On 9 February we had a tough mission to Magdeburg, Germany. I didn't

Mal Horton III, first pilot of the crew sharing our hut in 1945. He flew in the Battle of Britain with the RAF and then with our Air Forces in B-24s.

realize it at the time, but I was suffering from combat fatigue. Normal events became unreal. It was as if I were somewhere else, looking down on it all.

We flew again on 22 February, this time to Kriesen, Germany. We were hit by flak, sustaining some damage. Probably, I could have made it back to England, but I chose to go into a fighter strip near Liège. Then came the truck and Gooney ride back to England again. We were dropped off at an RAF base in the Midlands and returned to our base by truck.

I went to the Club and was having a drink when Colonel Westover, our Group Commander, approached me. He said, "I'm grounding you and sending you home. You and your bombardier have flown enough. You were the only ones who came back to our Group to fly second tours. We have enough crews now. I've called the 8th Air Force, and they said it was strictly up to me how many missions you fly. I don't want to see you guys get killed at this stage. The war is almost over. It *is* over for you two." I was angry at first. I believed I could fly more. But reflecting on it, it was probable that he had saved my life. I told Art. He had one less mission than I and did not want to quit until we were even.

We roomed with a crew whose Commander, Mal Horton III, had flown for the RAF in the Battle of Britain and in North Africa. He had transferred to our Air Force when we entered the war and now was flying a tour in B-24s. Art talked to him about wanting to fly one more mission. The Commander's crew was flying the next day, so Art went, putting him even with me in number of missions flown. He was then content to quit.

When the war had broken out, countries such as Holland, Belgium, France, Norway, and Poland had ships on the high seas that put into England rather than surrender to the Germans. Many crewmen aboard those ships joined the RAF. When the RAF wanted to hit a specific target in one of those countries, a crew native to that country and familiar with the particular target area flew the mission. The contributions of those brave men were legendary. We felt honored to meet them, and it was fun to enjoy a night at the bar with them. They were in for the duration. Many married English girls and had families.

No matter how much you flew or endured, you could always find someone who had endured more. I learned that war is not glamorous or glorious. It is death, destruction, blood, sweat, and tears. It is mud, misery, and suffering.

One truism I knew above all else — it had been a *sporty course*. Flying in the war was something I had to do, but it is something I want to see humankind avoid in the future. I had been lucky. Many men had not. All anyone can do is his job and then leave the rest up to God.

I don't believe God guides countries through wars. But I do believe he certainly guides individuals after they have done all in their power to accomplish their jobs. My military service had been the single most significant experience of my life. It would be years before I could sort it all out and

Celebrating finishing their second tour, Jack Swayze (left); his bombardier, Art Rayburn; Captain McCleary, his acting co-pilot; and Major Parks, a Group Officer (navigator) riding with the crew.

make sense out of all that had taken place. It would take years to answer all the questions I had and could not understand.

I knew I didn't want to leave — or more precisely, didn't want to leave flying. I had done too much living in that bird. I had seen too many live and far too many die to abruptly leave the Air Forces. It had become my life. After three years of war, I could not back off into peace and tranquility; war was still a part of me — and the world.

The war was raging in the Pacific at the time, and I volunteered for that duty. Until the Pacific conflict ended, the war was not over for the Armed Forces of the United States.

Chapter 17

In mid-March I flew from England to Prestwick, Scotland, on the way to my eventual reassignment from combat. There I boarded a flight for LaGuardia Airport in New York City. Just before leaving the base, new parkas had arrived for crew members. I was not about to chance losing mine, so I wore it.

I arrived in New York City wearing a combat parka, with combat binoculars hanging around my neck, and a .45 automatic in my shoulder holster. When I got off the plane I reported to the customs agent who said, "You don't have any government property, do you?"

I said, "No, Sir." He marked the sheet and had me sign it. That cleared my souvenirs.

A small Army Air Forces bus drove me to Fort Totten on Long Island where I received my orders to report to the Redistribution Center in Santa Monica, California, at the end of my leave. I had several days on the train to think. I wanted to go to B-29s and the Pacific. The war was still going there. I believed going to the Pacific might satisfy the need in me to see that all fighting stopped. I had no desire to be an instructor. But how would I explain all this to Jeri? She had never said no before to anything I felt would help my career.

Jeri came alone to meet me at the station. It was perfect. Then we went home to see the boys. They were no longer babies. My only disappointment was that they were wearing sailor suits!

I had been in combat for the past three years and Jeri had been alone, raising

Jack Werts, Mal Horton's bombardier.

our sons. Our finances had not allowed her the luxury of a washing machine, and she had washed by hand during those years. If there was a hero in our family, it was Jeri. She never complained. She patiently waited out the hours, days, years. She could do nothing but work and worry. At the Redistribution Center, Jeri would be able to enjoy herself and participate in fun activities in the Los Angeles area. Work would be done for her, instead of her doing for others.

We took the train to Los Angeles and a bus on to Santa Monica. We checked into the assigned hotel. Later in the day, we ran into Jack Werts, a bombardier from my Squadron, and his wife. We started seeing them. He was from Mal Horton's crew, which had shared our hut on the second tour. My bombardier had flown his last catch-up mission with them.

We also met Lieutenant Colonel Gill and his wife. Colonel Gill had been the officer in charge of the group returning to England after our earlier 30 days of Rest and Recuperation. It was good to see he had made it through his second tour. Colonel Gill flew with a B-17 Group. He and his wife lived in California. They had a car and took us with them to many places.

During our 10-day holiday in Santa Monica, we saw shows starring Danny Kaye, Ben Blue, and the Mills Brothers. The food was outstanding and so was the entertainment. It was fun, but it didn't last long enough.

When I reported in, I took tests and filled out many questionnaires. I always put down my desire to go to B-29s and the Pacific. When the orders came out, mine sent me to Enid, Oklahoma. I was to be an instructor in Advanced flight school for multi-engine cadets. I was to fly B-25s — that made no sense at all! I tried to get the orders changed, met a stone wall, and finally gave up.

We decided that Jeri should stay home until I had a permanent assignment, but I knew from the first minute I arrived at Enid that it would not work out. There were four of us who were returning B-24 drivers. I had come back from England, a Lieutenant had come back from Italy, and another Lieutenant and a Captain had arrived from the Pacific. Our orders were to replace personnel who had not yet seen combat. The base didn't want us; they weren't happy to see us.

On Monday morning of the second week, we reported to the Director of Operations office. We entered and took seats. A Major came in, telling us to stay seated. I knew something was up. He started his pitch: "I have instructed at Enid throughout the war. We have homes, families here. Now we are to replace ourselves. I am not going to replace myself. This base must provide pilots to the B-24 Replacement Training Unit at Charleston Army Air Field, South Carolina. We are not B-24 qualified. You four are not B-25 qualified but are B-24 qualified. We fly B-25s here. You have not checked out in the B-25, nor have you instructed. My decision is we ship you four to fill the need at the B-24 RTU."

Celebrating homecoming at the Florentine Gardens in Los Angeles with Jeri Swayze and the Jack Werts, the author is getting a hug from Sugar Geise.

Chapter 17

It was inevitable, and I knew it. What kind of deal would we receive if we tried to buck these people? And besides, I knew I would punch someone if I stayed at Enid, and my first victim probably would have been the Major. He handed us orders already prepared. The rotten opinion this gave me of the Training Command was to remain vivid in my memory for many years. Who would want to serve with such an officer?

We were on the road to Charleston by sunset and arrived there on VE Day — Victory in Europe — 9 May 1945. We ran into several officers in town who told us that all personnel had to remain on base that day and night; they suggested that we not check in until the next morning, which made sense to us. We registered at the Francis Marion Hotel and joined the festivities. It was fun in town that night.

Charleston was a Replacement Training Unit that had prepared B-24 crews for combat in Europe. But now that the war in Europe was over, there was no reason for the program to continue. We made a few training flights in B-24s with B-17 pilots, who were primarily returnees, shafted the same way we had been. They had orders as instructors and were to replace ones who had not been to combat as we had, then also ended up in Charleston.

We flew the B-24s to Ontario, California, and parked them at the Primary flight school I had attended where they became a part of the boneyard of planes left over from the war. We returned by train to Charleston, and upon our arrival, we could see several C-54s parked in front of base Operations.

I was on the schedule to take an instrument check in the C-54 the next day. It was not an ordinary instrument check, but one including an evaluation ride in the airplane. When we landed, I asked to see the Operations Officer who was a Captain. He seemed knowledgeable. I said, "What's in store for me? Why have I taken this check ride in the C-54?"

He took me into his office and told me they were checking pilots with 1,000 hours flying four-engine planes for assignment in C-54s. Those selected would go to Okinawa to support the invasion of Japan.

I blew my stack. I had just tried to go to the Pacific in B-29s and been ignored. Now someone wanted to send me in a transport for the invasion of Japan. I said, "I've just finished flying two tours of combat in Europe. Then I got sent to the Training Command. They shafted me to this base to avoid going themselves. I won't fly combat in an unarmed aircraft." Then I noticed that the Captain was not wearing any medals and asked, "Are you going to Okinawa?" He said he hadn't been asked, but that if he had been, he would go.

I replied, "I'm asking. You go and leave me here in your job."

He wanted to know what I really wanted to do. I told him, in jest, that I wanted to go to the Pacific Ferry Command in Long Beach, California. I left and heard nothing for a month. We spent our time roaming around, homesteading at "Folly Beach."

When word finally came, all unassigned officers were to report to the base theater. We went eagerly, hoping we might get some information. Orders were passed out for all of us. Mine were to the Ferry Command at Long Beach. I had mentioned Long Beach to the Captain in jest, but I was happy to be going there. Maybe I could get settled enough to have my family with me. My B-24 friends were also going to Long Beach, except for the Captain from the Pacific. He wanted out of the service so that he could go home to Freehold, New Jersey. He had no desire to stay in the Army Air Forces.

We were learning how things operated in the "land of the big PX." Truth became very illusive. In combat, we had lived by absolute truth. Combat was a matter of doing or not doing. There was no room for a lot of bull. Now it was anybody's guess what was going on. There were promises and stories, few of which were true.

I bought a Nash from a Navy man who was going overseas. He was a car dealer and had kept it in good shape. It was a coupe with two jump seats behind the front seat that would work out fine for the boys. When I arrived in Long Beach, I learned that the Pacific Ferry Command had been disbanded and had become the Pacific Division of the Air Transport Command.

Several of us with considerable multi-engine flying time received orders to attend the instrument school in Lubbock, Texas, where we received a good course in basic instruments. We flew in the T-6 trainer throughout the course, which I enjoyed. When I returned to Long Beach, I reported to a C-47 Squadron that would be flying millions of Army personnel back from the Pacific. We were scheduled for C-47 school, which was a two-week course. When I finished, I asked to see the Commander. I told him how long I had been away from home, wife, and family and said, "If I could count on being here some length of time, I would find a place to live and bring my family down." He told me I would be there for at least six months and probably a lot longer, so I decided to have them join me.

A married girlfriend of my wife's helped me locate an apartment. We found one right on the beach in Belmont Shores. The lady who owned it readily agreed to a six-month rental period, so I paid her a month's rent in advance.

I told the Commander I had found a place to live and wanted to go to Seattle to bring back my family. He approved the two-week leave I requested. I hoped the trip would take less time so that we could have a few days before I had to go back to work.

Jeri's aunt was visiting her sister in nearby Long Beach and wanted to return with me to Seattle. We drove straight through and made it in 33 hours. I picked up the family, drove back, and spent about a week in our new place. We loved the apartment. Living just across the street from the beach was a dream come true. We hoped for a long stay.

Monday morning came, and I went back to work. The day started with roll

Chapter 17

A cemetery in France of American servicemen killed in action.

Another cemetery in France for American servicemen who paid the price.

call. Names of those on orders to go elsewhere were read. I couldn't believe my ears: I was on the list to go to Fort Dix, New Jersey! I went to see the Commander. He was sympathetic but offered no solution. He said, "It's a shock to me, too."

I hurried home and told Jeri not to unpack anything else. Then I went to see the landlady. She was a doll, very understanding. She refunded the unused portion of our rent and wished us luck.

When we arrived at Fort Dix, I learned I would be flying a Gooney Bird. I asked for time to find a place for the family to live. We were staying in a motel and immediately started searching for a home. We looked all over, even crossing over into Pennsylvania, in search of a place to rent, then finally located a four-story row house at a price we could afford. It had four bedrooms, bath, living room, family room, dining room, and kitchen. There was also a summer kitchen on a closed-in back porch. The furnishings were old-fashioned but adequate. The doors were immense and made of solid wood. It would have taken a bulldozer to break into the house.

The change to peacetime, both for me personally and for the nations involved, was more complicated than anticipated. The treatment received at such bases as Enid certainly didn't help one's return to normalcy. But these experiences did present an astute understanding of the kind of injustice that could be met at the hands of those in power. The men who had not been to combat remained deathly afraid that they would lose their positions to combat returnees.

The nuclear end to the war in Japan had happened very quickly. Hiroshima and Nagasaki were too much for the Japanese warlords to handle. At the last minute, Russia had jumped in against Japan to get in on the spoils. They took the islands north of Japan and would have taken it all if MacArthur had allowed them to get away with it.

During this period we implemented the Marshall Plan to put both Europe and Asia back on a sound footing. The United States didn't want or take any territory. We tried to prevent a repeat of the mistakes made at Versailles after World War I, mistakes which ultimately led to World War II.

In the aftermath, I realized that the war had affected me more than I thought. I was restless. I couldn't settle down and had to be doing something all the time. I *thought* I was the same as before the war; I *wanted* to be the same as before the war. But I was not.

Still, after all these years, I have dreams at night. In my dreams I'm fighting the war over again. After more than 45 years of these dreams, I believe I'll forever remember those experiences.

Chapter 18

I checked in at Fort Dix, and they laughed when I presented my graduation certificate from the California Gooney Bird school. I was told that the Atlantic Division did not recognize Pacific Division schools. So it was back to school for two more weeks.

I reported to my work Squadron and found out that I would be flying as a copilot. The Squadron had its own first pilots. Squadron Operations scheduled each crew to fly every 13 days. Normally, a crew would fly to Nashville one day and bring a load back the next. We also flew to Newark, picked up about 30 returnees, and took them to Nashville. Another crew flew them on to Dallas. At Dallas, still another crew would take the flight to Long Beach. Then when a plane going the opposite direction arrived, we would fly it back to Newark. Our Squadron made 23 flights daily, and the airlines made 21 flights. Normally, we would make the trip in two days. Sometimes it would take an extra day to get a flight coming our way.

I had ten days off between flights. While off, I could do whatever I wanted as long as I stayed in the area and was available if needed — the exception was those times when I had to pull Officer of the Day or other details which were 24-hour shifts. We were finally a family again and looked forward to spending Christmas together for the first time.

On 21 December the weather was horrible when we landed in Columbus, Ohio, and we had to wait six hours for it to clear. When we arrived in Nashville, the weather was even worse, and because of it, no flights were coming our way from the West. Our crews were backlogged; many ahead of us also waited to go home.

We called Fort Dix and were told that if we could hitchhike on a flight, we could go on back. There was a flight that night. We tried to get the crew to let us sandbag, but they refused. We climbed on board anyway, figuring they wouldn't refuse to take off. We got home on Christmas Eve.

That Christmas meant more to me than any I had ever experienced. It was really something with our own turkey and trimmings. The boys with their toys were a delight. I had purchased some steel models of tanks and trucks from the base — surplus troop training equipment that there was no need for. They were virtually indestructible, making them perfect for the boys. I, too, was a boy again. Seeing them happy meant more than anything that possibly could have happened to me. It was our happiest Christmas ever — we were together.

On days off, Jeri and I went to shows and had fun times with our sons. Sometimes we visited historical places. We saw where Washington crossed the Delaware River and visited many historical areas surrounding Trenton. We stayed busy and happy.

I didn't like the C-47, however, because of my experiences with it during the war. I didn't consider an airplane safe if it had less than four engines!

Spring came, and most of the troops were home. Air Transport Command decreed that only those pilots with more than 1,000 hours in passenger aircraft could fly as crew members. That ended flying for all of the old bomber pilots.

My orders came to move to Stockton, California. I tried to find out about the mission there and learned that the base had housed German prisoners of war who had worked on farms in the area. At the war's end, however, the United States had shipped most of the prisoners home.

I was concerned about the condition of the tires on our Nash; it would be a long, hard trip, and they were pretty badly worn. I found a set through a highway patrolman; the tires were new and of good quality, and I got them at a discount! I was lucky.

We met a couple to take over the house; they lived with us the last two weeks. The landlady didn't lose a day's rent. The major was an Administrative Officer at the hospital at Fort Dix, and his wife was an Army nurse. They were quality people, and we had fun together.

While at Fort Dix, I had applied for a commission in the Regular Army. When I met the Evaluation Board, the President of it was the General who had asked for my hat during the war. Meeting with this Board convinced me that the war really had ended.

The Pentagon had not yet determined who would receive Regular Army commissions. Much work remained before peace would reign. The fighting had stopped and peace was replacing war, but it could not really end until all the fighting men were home in permanent billets. Fort Dix had not qualified as a normal peacetime assignment. That would come in the future.

The war would live vividly in the minds of veterans for a long time, as only those who experienced the horror of combat can tell you. I knew I needed to dismiss the war and everything it stood for, but total dismissal would not be possible. Continuing to live, however, would. The sporty course of combat inevitably became only memories and history. We entered a new phase of our lives.

Chapter 19

In mid-March 1946, we headed for Seattle where I would leave the family before going on to Stockton. We didn't have permanent antifreeze, only the alcohol-type, so many mornings the water in the radiator was mushy. I didn't think the cold had damaged the engine, however, because it was running quite well.

We were on the Pennsylvania Turnpike, approaching Bedford, when the engine made a loud noise. We nearly suffocated from the smoke and fumes entering the car. I knew then that the problem was serious, but figured I should keep going as long as I could. I exited the turnpike at Bedford, and we limped into town at not more than five miles an hour. The engine was belching and booming, and the car was lurching. I came to the Mercury garage and pulled in, just as the engine died permanently. I talked to the shop manager, and he suggested we get a room in the hotel across the street. In the meantime, he would find out what was wrong with the car.

We learned the next morning that the cold weather had caused the engine block to crack, which had allowed water to seep into two cylinders. The pistons in those cylinders had collapsed and had scored the cylinder walls. The only remedy was to bore the block and install oversized pistons. Fixing it would take longer than we could wait. Having just returned from service in the Army himself, the shop manager understood our problem and was sympathetic. He told us about a customer awaiting delivery of a new Mercury who was trading in an old Packard. He expected the man to be coming in with it right away. He would sell us the Packard at the low book price and do the boring on our Nash at no charge. That was far more than I had expected, so I told him to look into the Packard.

He made the arrangements and brought the car for us to see. It was very rusty, and the tires were terrible, but I told him, "We have a deal, providing you install the Nash's tires on the Packard." He agreed. I gave him $200 cash; he would wait for the balance until I reached Stockton and got paid. If nothing else went wrong, we would have enough money to complete the trip.

Later that day, we were on the road again. We made up a bed in the back by leveling the pile of gear and putting the bedding on top so that the boys could sleep when they grew tired of playing games. We had not been on the road an hour when I discovered that the radiator was leaking. We could drive only 15 minutes before it had to be refilled. The boys carried Boy Scout canteens, so when I found a stream alongside the road, I filled their canteens and took the water up to the car. Between that procedure and service stations, we managed to keep going.

We stopped early that night at a motel in the Pittsburgh area. Service stations had closed down, and it was too dark to see streams from the road. I knew I could fill the radiator in the morning with water from the room.

I stopped for water the next day at a service station in Wheeling, West Virginia. The man said he could reverse-flush the radiator, put in liquid solder, and solve the problem. I was desperate, so I agreed. The flushing only made the holes larger, and the solder ran out. We still had to keep going from station to station.

We arrived about noon in Canton, Ohio, where I found a Packard garage and stopped to see what they could do to help us. The service manager said, "Not much."

A mechanic said, "I saw a radiator core stored on the top of the office. It might fit your car." It did, and it was brand-new. In 1945, that was providence! The manager thought he could have the car ready in about three hours, and suggested we go to a show. The car was fixed when we came back from the movie, and we decided to drive all night.

At about 0200, in the middle of Indiana, we were getting low on gas. All of the gas stations I'd seen were closed. The gauge hit empty, and the engine quit. I put the car in neutral and hoped and prayed we would come to a station before the car stopped completely. We coasted slowly around a bend and there it was — an open station. We were barely moving as we coasted in. It was the Lord helping again.

A tank of gas renewed our spirits and sustained us through the night. We arrived in Cheyenne, Wyoming, the following evening. It was snowing, and the plows were just starting to clear the roads. We followed one all the way into

Laramie, then stopped to eat. We worried that night about getting stuck because we didn't have tire chains. Snow treads were unheard of at that time.

Jeri and I were getting tired and needed a rest. The boys were fine because they had slept in the bed in the back. About four in the morning, we drove into Montpelier, Idaho, where we found a hotel and rented a room. Then I went back outside and drained the radiator because we had no antifreeze and the water would freeze quickly as cold as it was.

We slept for four hours, then got up. We were making good time with the new radiator. The car was a good one, other than the rusty parts. We were driving on roads that had not been maintained during the war years. There were deep potholes, and I hit most of them. The old car took a beating. The windshield wipers started when we hit a pothole, then stopped when we hit the next one. The same was true for the horn. It blew and stopped with alternate bumps. The muffler had fallen off, and the remaining section of tail pipe was dragging on the road. When we reached Gooding, Idaho, late in the afternoon, we noticed that the back license plate was missing. It apparently had jarred loose and fallen off.

We found a service station in Gooding with a mechanic on duty. He wired up the exhaust pipe so that it wouldn't drag, and removed the horn wires so it wouldn't blow. That made travel more livable.

We arrived in Seattle tired and dirty but happy. The boys had gotten to know their dad for the first time, and I would spend a few days in Seattle before boarding the train for Stockton.

The program to release men from the service was accelerating. I have forgotten how many points it took to get out. I know I had enough for ten people, but I didn't want to be out. I wanted to stay in and fly for Uncle Sam. With the war in the Pacific over, Captains drove garbage trucks, did road and ground maintenance, and performed a variety of jobs.

We were sitting around at Stockton one day while the remaining German prisoners were cleaning and straightening the room. One was laughing. An American officer asked, "What's the joke?"

The German said, "This time the German makes your bed. The next time you make the Russky bed."

We kept hoping there would be a mission for the base. At first there had been a few C-47s for us to fly, but they had been put in storage. If we wanted flying time, we were on our own. We begged for flights at Fairfield, Hamilton, and other bases. Another officer and I went to Hamilton Air Field. The Operations Officer let us have an air/sea rescue B-17. We flew up and down the coast from San Francisco to Los Angeles for 12 hours. We made just one landing. Neither of us had landed a B-17 before with a boat attached to the bottom. Most of the time while in California I flew in a C-54 with a military airlift crew at Fairfield.

I realized I would have to apply for training of some type in order to get a decent job after release from the service. I had been working in the base Post Office. All I did was look up the addresses of personnel who had left and forward their mail to them. A Captain in Headquarters had placed my name on the list to go to the Adjutant General school at Fort Oglethorpe, Georgia, for training in administration. The school was for Army as well as Air Forces personnel. But first I got a few days off and went up to Seattle. My dad would be getting a new Chrysler soon, and he agreed to sell me his old one. He would use my Packard until his new car arrived.

On the way to the school at Fort Oglethorpe, I drove through Chattanooga, Tennessee. The school was just across the state line in Georgia.

Only a few of the students were fliers. I met another officer there who needed flying time for pay purposes. He knew someone based at Marietta who would let us fly a T-6.

On one of our long weekends, we drove to Marietta, flew the T-6, and returned late in the evening. We went to the downtown Officers Club that night. When we arrived, the party had been going on for quite awhile. The degree of inebriation got pretty high, so we started home. I was driving, and there were four of us in my car. The two officers in the back started riding me about how slow my Chrysler was. I picked up speed and was driving too fast. I thought I was on the street leading to the Fort, but I wasn't. The street went over a rise and dead-ended at a golf course. I couldn't stop, and I hit the stone wall bordering it.

I finished the school in bandages. The damage to my car couldn't be fixed before it was time for me to leave, so I sold it to the Company Commander.

I had been a fool. My dad never forgave me for wrecking that car. My wife accepted it, but she didn't like it. If I hadn't been stoned, I would not have driven so fast.

When I got back to Stockton, most of the people had left. Those still there were packaging everything on the base for shipment. We knew they were closing the base. I worked for awhile bringing records up to date, but I couldn't stand being without my family. That was all I wanted. I had a lot of leave time due, so I put in for a couple of weeks off and went home to Seattle. I had grown tired of pilot pools, morning roll calls, and nonsensical trivia.

When I returned to the base, I moved into the Visiting Officers Quarters. The building where I used to live had been closed. Shortly after my return, the Officer of the Day woke me up one morning at about 0200 and said he had my transfer orders. A staff car was outside to take me to Fairfield to catch the daily courier flight across the U.S. He didn't know my destination; he just knew I had to hurry or I'd miss the flight.

I made the plane and found that I was to get off in Kansas and take a connecting flight to Sherman, Texas. My assignment was to learn how to teach the Reserve Officers' Training Corps program at universities. I hadn't applied for it, but was selected because I had a college degree. After I had left for war, my wife had submitted my thesis to the Dean of our college. I had completed my class work and had written a draft of my thesis before I left; I had been granted my degree.

The ROTC school did wonders for my morale. I would be able to get a real assignment, and we could be together again as a family. All during the training course, I kept thinking about being placed at a university in the Northwest. The smart ones wrote the university of their choice requesting assignment. I knew nothing about such an approach. When the assignment lists arrived, all of the Northwest schools had requested officers by name. All the remaining universities with openings were in the South and East.

I almost chose the University of Alabama, but I had heard that Tuscaloosa was a small town, and finding housing in small towns could be a problem. Boston University also was on the list. I didn't believe a city that size would have a housing shortage, so I chose Boston. I was told to finish school, return to Stockton, and await orders.

Chapter 20

Only seven people remained at Stockton when I returned. They were shipping the last loads of government supplies and property. Then they, too, would leave and the base would be closed.

My orders for Boston University were due any day. I sent a request to the 1st Air Force in New York to authorize me a 30-day delay en route. I took a week to go to Seattle to pick up my family. We visited all the relatives, including my parents, who were then living in Seattle. I negotiated with Dad to let me have the old Packard back to make the trip to Boston. His new car had just arrived. We drove back to Stockton and picked up my orders to Boston; the orders allowed me the 30-day delay.

We decided to take the southern route to avoid as much ice and snow as we could. Other than damage from rust, the old Packard was still a real "going" machine. We spent Christmas Eve in a little town in Alabama. The people there set off fireworks for Christmas, a new experience for us. We spent Christmas night in the Poinsettia Hotel in Greenville, South Carolina. They served an excellent meal, and we enjoyed it. The next day we went on to the Naval Academy and spent a day and night with Jeri's cousin and her husband, Harold, who was a marine and taught there.

We arrived in Boston on 28 December. We registered in the Kenmore Hotel near Boston University, then began a search for a house. On our way to Boston, many people had told us that New Englanders were unfriendly. We found the exact opposite to be true. The people we communicated with went out of their way to be helpful.

We were paying $25 a day to stay in the hotel. At that rate, we would go broke in about a week. We learned about a winterized summer house available in Hough's Neck, and decided to investigate. The listing said, "No Children." I talked to our boys. I stressed to them our need of a house. They would have to behave as perfect gentlemen while we were there. The owner liked my wife and felt sorry for us; she rented us the house.

It was a small place on Hingham Bay, with shingles on the sides as well as on the roof. We loved it, even painted barn red. There were two bedrooms and a bath upstairs, with a combined living room, kitchen, and dining area on the main floor. It rented furnished for $65 a month, which sure beat $25 a day at the Kenmore. We became the happiest family in all of New England.

I went to the Army base the very next day to draw my pay and travel reimbursement. I had been a long time without a payday. An Air Forces Major was standing by as I finished my paperwork. Then he came over and introduced himself as the Liaison Officer for the First Army.

He told me I was in a lot of trouble because the Army Colonel at Boston University had been driving everyone nuts trying to track me down. The Colonel had been complaining to everyone almost daily; he thought I should have arrived in September, and he wanted to charge me with desertion. This scared me some. It didn't pay to start a job on a sour note, especially when you're working with all new personnel under a new Commander.

On 2 January, I went to the university almost at first light. I was waiting when the First Officer, an Army Lieutenant Colonel, arrived. He said, "Show no surprise at anything the Colonel says or does when he comes in. I'm the Executive Officer. Your Commander, Major Wiley, will be in shortly."

Major Wiley then came in and greeted me. He said, "Don't worry about the Army Colonel. You work for me. I'll make out your effectiveness report."

When the Colonel arrived, I went to his door and knocked. I entered the office, saluted, and introduced myself. I told him where I had been, and he said, "Can I do anything to help you?" That was it.

I was not in shock, but all the others were. They couldn't believe what had happened. I was glad they had been wrong. The Colonel did make me teach some Army classes, though I knew nothing about the subjects.

We had never received better treatment than we did in Boston. Everyone made us feel welcome. No one in our area had much money, but we shared what we had and gave each other help and friendship. New England has beautiful fall colors. A ride around old Route 128 was always a treat, as was a trip into New Hampshire. We loved the Northeast's different seasons and looked forward to each.

While the war had left me tense and easy to anger, affecting me more than I cared to admit at the time, the only cure would be family life and time. Nothing else would resolve the imbalance that combat had created in me. This assignment would help me adjust.

Many veterans had enrolled at Boston University and were enrolled in ROTC to get commissions. Some wanted to fly and make it a career. Others were still not sure what they wanted to do with their lives. Our job was to present the pros and cons of military service. We were to help them decide what was correct for them. I made it plain. Someone with connections who could join a family firm with a good salary should do so. I told the young men up front that they would be foolish to come in to the military unless they were sure they desired a military career. Some did join and were happy and successful.

There were many young men at the university who hated the military. Some were veterans and most were instructors. On the whole, they made me angry. Many professors made only negative remarks about the military and the war. They didn't know anything about it, but they had a lot to say. Thank God for the professors who knew the truth and were supportive.

I eventually found out what had bothered the Colonel about my coming. It was the Effective Date for Change of Morning Report (EDCMR). My orders originally had a September date for EDCMR. But they had been a month late in arriving at Stockton. No one had told Boston University of my approved delay en route. The EDCMR date is set by the losing Command and is just a date to change reporting, not a date of arrival at the next duty station. On that date, the old Command drops the individual from its morning report and the new Command picks him up. I suspect the Colonel knew a lot more than he ever let on about the affair. He loved to give junior officers a hard time. It was his way of educating the younger ones.

An example was Norm, the Executive Officer, a Lieutenant Colonel. The Colonel put his desk at the far end of the office area. Then he would shout and make Norm come running. And it embarrassed Norm when the Colonel came out and talked to lower-ranking people and ignored him. But this was all part of the "education."

We often went to the cafeteria for coffee during the mid-morning break. We flipped a coin to see who would pay. At five cents a cup, no one got hurt. The Colonel declined to join in as that was gambling with junior officers and was against his West Point experience. Actually, he was technically correct; and he was doing it only to make a point.

Two of the four Air Force officers held ratings as pilots. We flew at Bedford Field north of Boston. Regulations allowed us one day a week. Out of courtesy, we had to clear each flight with the Colonel; it was always a show. We would go in, salute, and inform him we were going flying.

"Do you know how to fly?" he would ask.

Chapter 20   145

"We must keep training to stay proficient," we answered.

He would say, "I don't understand the need to train for something you already know how to do." The banter usually went on for a good 15 minutes. He would then say, "All right, go fly. You postmen stop bothering me."

Past events had shaped this man. He was probably the only Colonel from the class of 1914 who had not made General. He had been the Commander of a crack infantry regiment when the war broke out. He took them to the port where the Army relieved him of command for being too old. It hurt him, and he never recovered.

In spite of his peculiarities, he was a fine officer. I learned much from him. He always made sure we passed inspections. He was thorough and ensured that we followed regulations to the letter.

Eventually I became entrenched in the university. Finally, I relaxed and believed the war was over. Mission briefings were an item from the past. No more bombs to drop. No more flak to fly through. No more burning airplanes to watch while hoping some of the crew would bail out. It was time to celebrate. It was time to live as a human being again. This was a four-year assignment, time to assess all that had taken place in the war years. It was a glorious feeling.

Epilogue

The 2nd Air Division flew its first mission on 7 November 1942, the last on 25 April 1945. The crews of the 2nd flew a total of 95,948 sorties. The B-24s participated in 439 bombing missions, dropping a total of 199,983 tons of bombs. The Division's bomber crews shot down 1,079 German fighter aircraft; its P-38s, P-47s, and P-51s destroyed another 3,670 enemy aircraft in the air and on the ground. The 2nd Air Division lost a total of 1,458 bombers and 649 fighters during bombing operations.

I am proud to have participated, particularly to have been a volunteer. I am also proud to have lost no one flying with me nor any of our Group crews when I flew lead.

In 1947 when the Army Air Forces became the United States Air Force, a separate service from the Army and the Navy, I joined as an original Regular officer. I received a Regular Army commission in the second integration.

I served my full career with my first assignment in ROTC at Boston University, then to Germany for four years, which proved interesting and allowed us to visit much of Europe. I came back to attend Air Staff and Command School at the Air University in Montgomery, Alabama, and afterward I served a tour in Maryland in the Research and Development Command at Aberdeen Proving Ground. My work there was supporting weapons development by the Army Chemical Corps and the Army Ordnance Corps.

Epilogue

From there I had a long tour in Tucson, Arizona, where I flew B-47 bombers. It was a pleasure to get back into the cockpit again. When the Air Force retired the B-47s, I went into missiles with a tour in the Atlas ICBM program at Cheyenne, Wyoming. From there I went to Grand Forks, North Dakota, to be part of the Minuteman II program. My final assignment was with ROTC again, this time at the University of Montana, from which I retired.

Index

by Lori Daniel

1st Air Division, 57
1st Air Force, 142
First Army, 114, 143
2nd Air Division, 57, 146
3rd Air Division, 57
8th Air Force, 41, 65, 67, 73, 77, 83, 87-89, 91, 108, 110-111, 115, 123
    Accident Board, 67
9th Air Force, 66, 73, 91, 111, 121
9th Armored Division, 99
Ninth Corps, 2
19th Bombardment Group, 32
44th _____, 104
82nd Airborne Division, 105
93rd _____, 104
101st Airborne Division, 105
448th Bomb Group, Heavy, 34-35
446th Bomb Group, 34
715th Squadron, 82

— Aircraft —

AT-9, 17-18
AT-17 bamboo bomber, 17-18
B-17 Flying Fortress, viii, 2, 19-23, 25-26, 28-29, 31-32, 55, 57-58, 67, 74, 85, 89, 112, 127, 129, 139
B-24 Liberator, viii, 29, 32-34, 38, 45, 53, 55, 57-60, 67, 74-75, 78-79, 82, 89, 103-106, 112, 114, 122-123, 127, 129-130, 146
    Davis wing, 29
B-24E, 38
B-24H, 38, 43
B-24J, 58
B-24 RTU, 127
B-25, 41, 127
B-26, 66, 91, 94, 100
B-29, 125, 127, 129
B-47, 147
British Halifaxes, 91
British Lancaster bomber, 88
British Meteors, 107
BT-13 Vultee Vibrator, 12
BT-15, 12
C-47 Gooney Bird, 105, 112-114, 121, 123, 130, 133, 135, 139
C-54, 129, 139
FW-190, 71, 104
Heinkel, 115
ME-109, 75, 120
ME-163, 107

ME-262, 71, 107, 115
ME-263, 71
P-38 Lightning, 2, 6, 13, 43, 146
P-47 Jug, 70, 78, 146
P-51, 120, 146
PT-13, 9
PT-17, 9-10
Stearman, 9-10
T-6 trainer, 130, 140

— A —

Africa, 43, 46, 53
    Dakar, 41, 43-44
    Sahara Desert, 44
Air Defense Command, 108
Air Transport Command, 130, 135
    Pacific Division, 130
Air Training Command, 120
Alabama, 142
    Montgomery, 146
        Air University, 146
            Air Staff and Command School, 146
    Tuscaloosa, 141
        University of Alabama, 141
Alaska, 2
Allies, 5, 17, 86-87, 107, 110-111, 114-115
America, 16, 49
American, viii, 3, 5, 8, 30, 44, 46, 49-50, 57, 64, 66, 68, 87, 90, 93, 95, 98, 107, 111, 113, 115, 131-132, 139
Arizona
    Bixby, 16
    Douglas, 16
    Phoenix, 16
    Tucson, 16, 147
Ascension Island, 43
Asia, 133
Atlantic, 47, 70
    North, 38
Atlas Mountains, 44-45
Australian, 98
Aviation Cadet, 16
    program, 2, 4
        Advanced training, 13, 16, 18, 20, 28, 40
        Basic training, 12-13, 16
        First pilot, 26, 28, 34
        Instrument flying, 13
        Navigation School, 34
        Pre-flight training, 6, 9
        Primary training, 9-11, 16, 18

Index

AWOL, 29

— B —
Battle of Britain, 122-123
Battle of the Bulge, 111, 114
Belgium, 113, 123
  Brussels, 81, 112-113, 121
Billings, Charlie, 73-74, 85-86
Bird Dog (radio compass), 43, 48
Black, Captain, 58, 76-77
Blue, Ben, 127
Boeing, 55
Boutelle, Sperling, 2
Bradley, General Omar, 114
Brazil
  Belem, 41-42
  Natal, 41-42
  Rio de Janeiro, 42-43
Britain, 3, 49, 68
British, 16, 49-50, 53, 60, 78-79, 87-88, 98-99, 107, 112-113
  Bomber Command, 91
British Guyana
  Georgetown, 41-42
Broxten, Hervey, 71
Bruce _____, 108
Bulova, Walt, 69
Burcham, Milo, 18

— C —
California, 6, 8, 16, 19, 35, 127, 139
  California Valley, 12
  Cosmolene, 19
  Fairfield Field, 139-140
  Gooney Bird school, 134
  Hamilton Field, 139
  Laguna Beach, 8
  Lancaster, 12-13
    War Eagle Field, 12
  Long Beach, 129-130, 134
    Pacific Ferry Command, 129-130
  Los Angeles, 8, 127, 128, 139
    Florentine Gardens, 128
  Mojave, 15
  Mojave Desert, 12
  Ontario, 9, 12, 129
    Cal Aero Academy, 9
    Primary flight school, 129
  Puente, 10
  San Francisco, 2, 139
  Santa Ana, 5-6, 8, 11
    Pre-flight Training Center, 6
  Santa Monica, 125, 127
    Redistribution Center, 125, 127
  Stockton, 135, 137-142, 144
Cheyenne Agency, 36
Civil Service, 2-3
Class 43-E, 26-27
Colorado
  Denver, 27
  Wallula Gap, 27
Connecticut, 37
Control Point
  "A," 85, 103

Control Point *(continued)*
  "B," 103
Convair, 55, 58

— D —
D-Day invasion, 87
DDT bomb, 41, 43
Distinguished Flying Cross, 101-102
Doolittle, Lieutenant General James, 67, 89
Dorsey Brothers, 90
Dutch, 106

— E —
Effective Date for Change of Morning Report (EDCMR), 144
Einstein, Albert, 60
Engines
  Jacobs, 10
  Lycoming, 10
  Pratt and Whitney, 12, 32, 37, 43
  Wright, 12, 15, 32
England, 40, 45-50, 55, 64-66, 69-70, 72, 74, 78, 83, 86, 90, 98-99, 104, 106, 108, 113, 115, 117, 121, 123, 125, 127
  Coventry, 87
  Ilfracombe, 69
  London, 54, 56, 64, 66, 75, 83, 85, 87-88, 107, 117
    Regent Palace Hotel, 117
  Newquay, 41, 48
  Norwich, 50
  Seething, 41, 50, 52, 76, 81, 114
  Southampton, 100
  Watton, 50, 53
    Depot, 50, 53
English, 44, 49, 64, 79, 98, 123
English Channel, 55, 58, 60, 65, 68, 71, 76, 78-79, 82, 85, 103-105, 112-114
Europe, 32, 57, 87, 91, 110, 129, 133, 146

— F —
Florida, 78
  West Palm Beach, 38, 40, 45, 64
Ford Motor Company
  Willow Run Plant, 58
Fortress Europe, 72, 91
France, 55, 102, 123, 131-132
  Beauvoir, 85
  Dieppe, 65
  Fecamp, 83
  Mozenville, 76
  Paris, 83-84
  St. Pierre de Jongurer, 60
  Sira Court, 83
  Versailles, 133
  Watten, 76
  Woippy, 85
Free-French, 45
French, 98
  coast, 65, 86
French Foreign Legion, 45
French Guyana, 42
  Devil's Island, 42

French Morocco
  Marrakech, 41, 44-47
    Mammonia Hotel, 45-46
    Sultan's Palace, 46

— G —

Geise, Sugar, 128
General Dynamics, 55
Georgia, 140
  Fort Oglethorpe, 140
  Marietta, 140
German, 16, 45, 47-48, 55, 57, 59-60, 62, 65, 68-69, 71-76, 78-81, 83, 86-88, 90, 92-93, 95, 98, 104-105, 107-108, 110-111, 113-114, 117, 123, 135, 139, 146
  Luftwaffe, 41, 70, 73, 75, 81, 107
    Abbeyville Kids, 81, 104
Germany, 3, 47, 60, 65, 70, 73, 75-76, 79, 82, 87, 107, 114-115, 117-120, 146
  Berlin, 74-75, 81, 89, 103-104
    Erkner Werks, 74
  Bielefeld, 109
  Bohlen, 83
  Bremen, 53
  Clausthal K, 107
  Cologne, 108
  Dresden, 120
  Dumar Lake, 104
  Ehrang, 111
  Frankfurt, 65-67, 75, 108-109
  Furth, 73
  Gotha, 72
  Hamburg, 74, 87
  Hamm, 77, 106
  Hanau, 111
  Kaiserslautern, 55, 111
  Kilchberg, 120
  Koblenz, 83, 107-108
  Kriesen, 123
  Liège, 123
  Ludwigshaven, 55
  Magdeburg, 121
  Mannheim, 80
  Manston, 107, 114
  Meppen, 60
  Mulhouse, 83
  Neinberg, 74
  Neunkirchen, 110
  Oranienburg, 103
  Peenemünde, 115
  Pforzheim, 106
  Ruhr, 83, 120
    Dortmund, 120
    Muenster, 83
  Tutow, 83
  Zundberg, 60
Gibraltar, 98
Gill, Lieutenant Colonel, 100, 127
Grable, Lieutenant Colonel John, 102, 114
Ground Control, 15, 66, 69
  school, 22

— H —

Harmon, Tom, 41

Hawaii
  Pearl Harbor, 1, 3, 32
Hesepe raid, 71
HF (high frequency), 38, 48
Hitler, Adolph, 108, 114-115
Holland, 71, 105, 123
  Groesbeek, 105
Hoover, Don, 13
Horton III, Mal, 122-123, 126-127

— I —

Idaho, 30, 34
  Boise, 29-31
    Gowan Field, 29-33
  Gooding, 139
  Montpelier, 139
Illinois
  Chicago, 34, 94-95
  Peoria, 34, 94
Indian, 20, 34
Indiana, 138
Initial Point (IP), 55, 67, 73, 75, 89
Iowa, 44
  Sioux City, 34
Ireland, 91
Italian, 98
Italy, 3, 40, 73, 98, 127

— J —

James, Harry, 90
Japan, 1, 3, 32, 115, 129, 133
  Hiroshima, 133
  Nagasaki, 133
Japanese, 1, 3, 16, 133
  American, 3
Jews, 90
Joshua tree, 13
Jutland Peninsula, 103-104

— K —

K-24 camera, 73, 104
Kansas, 18, 140
  Herington, 38
Kaye, Danny, 127
Kentucky
  Fort Knox, 99
King George, 50

— L —

Leonard, Major General, 100
Lincoln, Abraham, 52
Lindbergh, Charles, 43
Lockheed, 13
Lord Haw Haw, 90
Lothar, Captain, 94

— M —

MacArthur, Douglas, 133
Manhattan, 93
Marshall Plan, 133
Maryland
  Aberdeen Proving Ground, 146
Mason, Colonel, 77, 80

Index

Massachusetts
  Bedford Field, 144
  Boston, 92, 142-144
    Harbor, 94
    Kenmore Hotel, 142
    University, 141-144, 146
      ROTC, 146
  Camp Miles Standish, 94
  Hingham Bay, 143
  Hough's Neck, 143
  Kenmore, 143
McCleary, Captain, 124
Mess, 40, 50, 53, 69, 77, 80, 93, 98
  card, 31, 34
  kits, 45
Mexico
  Agua Prieta, 18
Michigan, 41
Mickey Operator (navigator), 106, 112, 120
Midlands, 123
Midway Islands, 16
Military Police (MP), 34, 41, 46
Miller, Glenn, 90
Mills Brothers, 127
Montana
  University of, 147
    ROTC, 147
Morse code, 17

— N —

Nazi, 111
Netherlands
  Arnhem, 105
New England, 142-143
New Guinea, 16
New Hampshire, 143
New Jersey
  Atlantic City, 94
    Redistribution Center, 95, 98
  Fort Dix, 133-136
  Freehold, 130
  Newark, 134
  Trenton, 135
New Mexico, 47
  Hobbs, 19, 20, 24, 26
  Las Vegas, 27
  Lovington, 23
New York, 6-7, 13, 98-99, 142
  Long Island, 125
    Fort Totten, 125
  New York City, 35, 94, 125
    Hotel New Yorker, 94
    Grand Central Station, 94
      Army Transportation Office, 94
    LaGuardia Airport, 125
Nissen hut, 50
Normandy, 83
North Africa, 13, 16, 123
North Carolina, 34
North Dakota
  Grand Forks, 147
    Minuteman II program, 147
North Sea, 60
Norway, 123

— O —

Ohio
  Canton, 138
  Columbus, 134
Okinawa, 129
Oklahoma, 35
  Enid, 127, 129, 133

— P —

Pacific, 16, 32, 40, 115, 124-125, 127, 129-130, 139
  South, 38, 43
Palm Inspection, 37
Parks, Major, 124
Pathfinder radar, 106, 108
Patton, General, 114
Pennsylvania, 28, 35, 133
  Bedford, 137
  Clark's Summit, 20
  Philadelphia, 3
  Pittsburgh, 138
  Scranton, 20
  Turnpike, 137
Poland, 123
Presidential Unit Citation, 106-107
PSP
  landing, 121
  runway (pierced-steel-planking), 43
Puerto Rico, 40-42
  Ramey Field, 40
PX, 130
Pyrenees, 98

— Q —

Queen Elizabeth, 99

— R —

Radio Berlin, 90
  "Berlin Betty," 90
Radio Bremen, 90
  "Midge," 90
R and R (Rest and Recuperation), 94, 127
Rayburn, Art, 92-95, 100, 105, 108-109, 121, 123-124
Red Cross, 87, 99
Rhode Island
  Providence, 94
River
  Amazon, 42
  Delaware, 135
  Missouri, 36
  Oronoco, 42
  Rhine, 55, 76-77, 105
Ross, Bill, 20, 28-29, 33-34, 57, 95, 98
Royal Air Force (RAF), 50, 68-69, 88, 122-123
Rumania
  Ploesti, 32
Russia, 133
Russian, 93
Rybos, Charlie, 7-8

— S —

Scotland
  Prestwick, 125

Singapore, 93
Skaggs, Captain, 78-79
South America, 41, 44
South Carolina
  Charleston, 34, 127, 129
    Army Air Field, 127
    B-24 Replacement Training Unit, 127, 129
    Francis Marion Hotel, 129
  Greenville, 142
    Poinsettia Hotel, 142
Spain, 98
Spanish, 98
  Main, 42
Spanish Morocco, 47
Stewart, Jimmy, 34
Stroud, Lieutenant Colonel, 105-106
Swayze
  family, 97
  Gordon Burriss, 19
  Jack, 49, 51, 80, 84, 96, 101, 114, 124, 128
  Jeri, 1, 4, 19, 28-30, 37, 42, 80, 95, 125, 127-128, 130, 134, 139, 142
Sweden, 86
Switzerland, 89
Swiss, 42

— T —

Tarrant, Moose, 72
Tennessee
  Chattanooga, 140
  Nashville, 134
Texas
  Belmont Shores, 130
  Dallas, 134
  Lubbock, 130
  Marfa, 17
  Piote, 19-20
  Sherman, 140
  Wink, 17
Tex Rankin's Flying Circus, 9
Theater
  European, 12, 115
  Pacific, 12
  Theater Change, viii
Third Reich, 110
Thompson submachine gun, 8
Timberlake, General, 109
Tokyo (auxiliary) tanks, 58, 65-67

— U —

United Air Lines, 2
United States, vii-viii, 3, 5-6, 16, 40-41, 68, 77, 86, 90, 93-94, 98-99, 120, 124, 133, 135, 140, 146
  Air Corps, 102
  Air Force, 146-147
  Armed Forces (Army Air Forces), 124
  Army, 4, 6-7, 9-11, 16-18, 20-22, 28, 34, 83, 94, 105, 130, 135, 137, 143, 145-146
    Air Forces, 28, 88-89, 91, 113, 122-125, 130, 143-144, 146
    Check Pilots, 9

United States *(continued)*
  Army *(continued)*
    Chemical Corps, 146
    Headquarters, vii, 26, 28, 32, 45, 47, 62, 67, 74-75, 78, 81, 83, 85, 88, 91, 102, 105, 107-109, 111, 140
    Horse Cavalry, 8
    Infantry, 8
    Intelligence, 67, 70-71, 74, 109
    Officers Club, 28-29, 33-34, 36, 41-42, 50, 53, 67, 70, 77, 102, 109, 123, 140
    Ordnance Corps, 146
    Squadron Operations, 13, 33-37, 39-40, 70, 74, 76, 102, 108, 112-114, 121, 127, 129
  Coast Guard, 93
  Congress, viii
  government, 64
  Marine Corps, 15
  Navy, 2, 16, 76, 130, 146
    Navy Special, 29-30
    Pacific Fleet, 3
  Regular Army, 135, 146
  ROTC, 141, 144
Utah
  Wendover, 35

— V —

V-1 rockets, 76, 107, 120
V-2 rockets, 69, 76, 107, 117
VE Day (Victory in Europe), 129

— W —

Washington, 6, 135
  Boeing Field, 2
    Quartermaster Depot, viii, 2-4, 58
  Ephrata, 29
  Everett, 2
    Paine Field, 2
  Kennewick, 4, 27, 96
  Moses Lake, 26-29
  Seattle, 2, 11, 18, 27, 95, 130, 137, 139-140, 142
  Spokane, 2, 28, 30
  Twin lakes, 97
  University of, 1
Washington, D.C.
  Pentagon, 62, 135
Waters, Ralph "Georgie," 50
Watson, Orlo, 9-11
Webb, Lieutenant Colonel, 104
Weider, "Full Boost," 21
Werts, Jack, 126-128
Westover, Colonel, 106, 108-109, 123
West Point, 144
West Virginia
  Wheeling, 138
Wiley, Major, 143
World War I, 5, 133
World War II, vii, 5, 13, 133
Wyoming
  Cheyenne, 138, 147
    Atlas ICBM, 147
  Laramie, 139